Wild Heart of Los Angeles

THE SANTA MONICA MOUNTAINS

Wild Heart

THE SANTA MONICA MOUNTAINS

# of Los Angeles

by Margaret Huffman

ROBERTS RINEHART PUBLISHERS

Published by Roberts Rinehart Publishers
6309 Monarch Park Place
Niwot, Colorado 80503

tel   303 · 652 · 2685   fax 303 · 652 · 2689

Distributed to the trade by Publishers Group West

Published in the UK and Ireland by
Roberts Rinehart Publishers
Trinity House, Charleston Road
Dublin 6, Ireland

PHOTOGRAPHY: Photographs by Margaret Huffman unless accompanied by other credits.
    List of other photography credits are found on page 193.

BOOK DESIGN AND PRODUCTION: Jim Mafchir/Western Edge Press

EDITOR: Robin Gould

FIGURES: Deborah Reade

International Standard Book Number 1-57098-172-8

Library of Congress Catalog Card Number 97-76498

10 9 8 7 6 5 4 3 2 1

Manufactured in Hong Kong

Contents

Preface   vii

1. PEOPLE, PLANTS, AND ANIMALS TOGETHER   3

2. CREATING THE RANGE   25

3. CHAPARRAL—PRODUCTIVE SURVIVOR   39

4. COASTAL AND INTERIOR SAGE SCRUB—ON THE BRINK   57

5. OAK WOODLAND AND VALLEY OAK SAVANNA—OLD CALIFORNIA   75

6. FRESH WATER—SHADY OASES   93

7. BY THE SEA   107

8. CALIFORNIA INDIANS—THE FIRST PIONEERS   119

9. EUROPEAN SETTLERS—THE CHANGERS   129

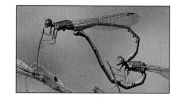

10. PEOPLE AND THEIR HANGERS–ON   141

11. MOUNTAINS AFIRE—DEATH AND REBIRTH   155

12. ALTERNATIVE FUTURES   173

References   179

Index   189

Photography Credits   195

Preface

IN 1953 I MOVED FROM THE EAST COAST TO LOS ANGELES. THERE, ONLY a few minutes' drive from my house, were the Santa Monica Mountains, with their open space and spectacular scenery. They made me feel free and adventurous, but the plants that covered their slopes seemed shriveled and alien.

One afternoon, while I was driving up a canyon road, a mountain lion suddenly appeared from out of the brush. I should have been frightened, but the animal seemed more like an overgrown, playful cat than a vicious predator, and for about a half-mile she frolicked alongside my car, like a dolphin sporting with a boat. That was enough to make me fall in love with the mountains. Since then, all of their moods, from gorgeous spring bloom to rampant wildfire, have engrossed me.

When I was a girl, and there was still open land in Rochester, New York, I went with my mother and dad for walks and picnics on the vacant hill near our house. Mother exclaimed over the beauty of butterfly weed in bloom; Dad showed me how robins had molded their nests of mud and grasses. By the time I was in the fifth grade, I was collecting butterflies and watching caterpillars wrap cocoons and come out later as elegant moths.

As soon as I was settled in Los Angeles, my love of nature drew me to the local chapter of the Audubon Society. At that time, Jim Huffman was chapter president and led local field trips. His love for birds, and delight in sharing them with others, attracted me, and, when he invited me for our own jaunt into the mountains, I was excited—not only by the prospect of seeing birds.

He found golden-crowned sparrows for me in Tapia Park (named for one of the early owners of the Malibu rancho), a Hutton's vireo in Tuña Canyon, seabirds that nest in the north spending the winter at Malibu Lagoon. He taught me what kinds of vegetation different birds like and how to tell apart the tiny voices of the warblers, and, later, showed me off to his bird-watching friends. For my birthday, he gave me a high-class pair of binoculars. Soon our bond was far stronger than our shared love of nature.

I took him to see my mountain lion, but someone had shot her, someone too mean-spirited to be excited by her wildness. Joy left me for a time; anger followed.

Married, Jim and I visited the wild lands all over California whenever our jobs allowed. We had fun introducing friends to our special spots and helping them share our pleasure.

One early spring, mountain flowers, coming into bloom, so entranced us we took a course on wildflower identification at UCLA. For three nights a week after work, we reveled in wildflower colors, forms, and aromas in a classroom. When we were through, we had even more places to go and things to share with others.

After that, I began to lead nature walks, often in the Santa Monica Mountains because I couldn't take the time from my job that extended trips demanded. The more I hiked in my mountains, the more I learned about them and loved them, and the more I saw how my knowledge and pleasure made children and adults alike, happy, too.

I also saw the many ways people were destroying the wilderness in my back yard. They were bulldozing the soaring ridges to turn them into pedestals for houses. They were yanking out the flowering shrubs our wildlife depend on and replacing them with toxic plants from other countries. They were leaving kittens and puppies unprotected, and poisoning the handsome coyotes that devoured their pets, not knowing that coyotes are essential to the health of our mountains.

In some ways, people hurt the mountains because they care too much for what the mountains offer—views, clean air, escape from urban pressures, being part of nature. It's also because most people aren't aware they can harm what they care for, even without meaning to.

When I retired, at last, this book was asking me to write it. I want it to encourage people—not just a few on an occasional nature walk, but many—to love my mountains. And I want to help people understand how what they do affects our Santa Monicas. I believe that people are more likely to slow, or even reverse, the destruction, if they know what they've been destroying and how they've been doing it—if they understand the wild heart of Los Angeles.

I describe plants and animals in terms of how they affect each other in their natural environment. Isolated descriptions of plants and animals are like dried botanical specimens and animals shut up in a zoo, as though a living thing exists in a self-contained paragraph. Though zoos have their place, an animal in a cage is like a man in prison, in the sense that the animal cannot behave in its own ways, the ways life has prepared it for.

Of course, no book can fully describe even a single plant or animal, but I've tried to catch some of the character of a living thing by telling stories about its relations with the others it lives with. Stories like these emphasize the ways plants and animals interconnect in the natural world.

There's room in this book to write about only a few of the many plants and animals in the Santa Monica Mountains. I've chosen animals from each of the classes, such as insects and reptiles, but especially birds and mammals. For the plants I've generally selected from those most common.

During most of the ten thousand years people have lived around and in the Santa Monicas, their effects on the mountains have been minor. I include California Indians and Spanish missionaries, because they fascinate, if only because they tell us about ourselves, and have colorful stories to be told. They also lead to Mexican rancheros, who began to destroy mountain plants and animals, and settlers from the East Coast, who hastened the destruction.

Decades of first-hand experiences are the foundation of this book. The experiences are my own and those of others who, like me, spend fair amounts of time in the mountains: Mark Bueller, Bob Burns, David Hollombe, Tom Keeney, Betsey Landis, Sean

Manion, Marian Peck, Margaret Stassforth, Ray Sauvajot, Tim Thomas, Mary Valentine, and Laurel Woodley.

First-hand experiences, however, can be misleading and, for an entire mountain range, must be incomplete. So ecologists, entymologists, historians, architects, mammalogists, geologists, and other specialists have patiently and generously helped me check facts and fill in where they have seen something missing. Among these specialists are Doug Allan, Brian Dillon, Pat Enkema, Art Evans, Don Franklin, Scott Franklin, Kimball Garrett, Lee Kats, Russ Kimura, Ruth Lebow, Sylvia Neville, Emil Sandmeier, Jan Timbrook, and Dave Pierpont. My thanks, too, to Deborah Reade, who produced the beautiful maps and figures and Robin Gould who ensured the clarity and suitability of the text. I'm especially indebted to Jim Mafchir for his artistic sense and skill in creating the format of the book.

The index includes scientific names for species mentioned. For example, when I talk about a dusky-footed woodrat, the index gives its name in two forms: woodrat, dusky-footed, and *Neotoma fuscipes.*

Margaret Huffman
Los Angeles

Wild Heart of Los Angeles

THE SANTA MONICA MOUNTAINS

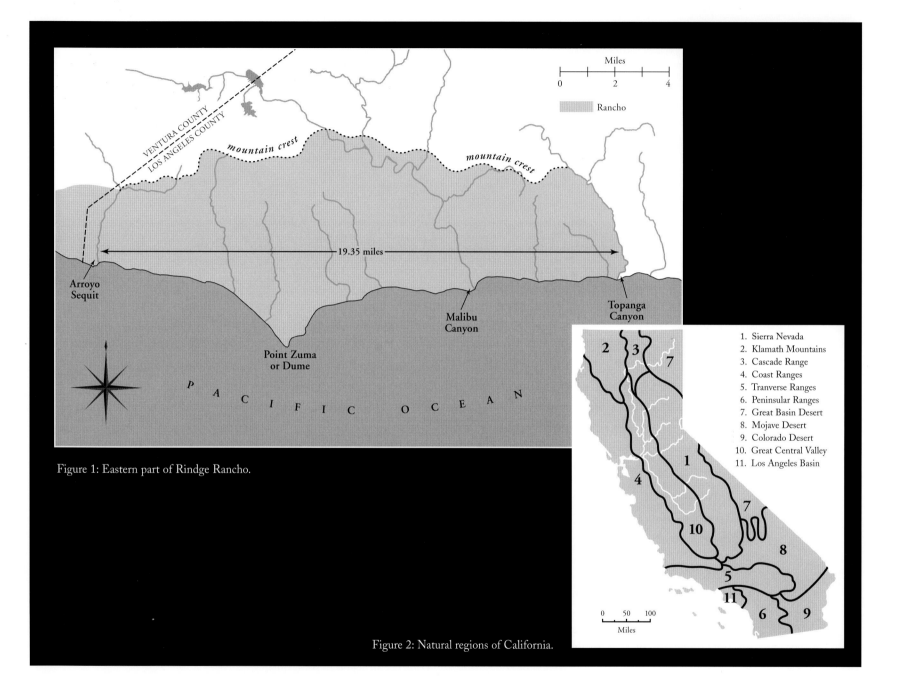

Miles
0   2   4

Rancho

VENTURA COUNTY
LOS ANGELES COUNTY

mountain crest   *mountain crest*

19.35 miles

Arroyo
Sequit

Malibu
Canyon

Topanga
Canyon

Point Zuma
or Dume

PACIFIC OCEAN

Figure 1: Eastern part of Rindge Rancho.

1. Sierra Nevada
2. Klamath Mountains
3. Cascade Range
4. Coast Ranges
5. Tranverse Ranges
6. Peninsular Ranges
7. Great Basin Desert
8. Mojave Desert
9. Colorado Desert
10. Great Central Valley
11. Los Angeles Basin

0   50   100
Miles

Figure 2: Natural regions of California.

CHAPTER 1

People, Plants, and Animals Together

ABOVE THE HEART OF *LOS ANGELES, THE SANTA MONICA MOUNTAINS PAINT A VISION*—now dark green, now misty lavender, now black and scattered with lights. Though the mountains seem remote from our urban pressures, we, and the plants and animals living around them and in them, affect each other in many ways, some dramatic, some strange, some comic.

This book focuses on the fascinating interactions among the climate, geology, topography, plants, and animals of the Santa Monica Mountains—the interrelatedness of life. Over the millennia, the players in these activities have evolved within ecosystems. I was tickled when I found out that "eco" comes from the Greek word, *oikos,* meaning household. So ecosystems are the households of nature—exactly my view of the goings-on in the Santa Monica Mountains.

As in a household, a network of interactions in an ecosystem allows plants and animals to fill their needs while they accommodate one another. How well the network does its many jobs depends on how easily plants and animals can contact each other (in a sense,

communicate with each other), as well as on the health of the ecosystem. Ecosystems that have many kinds of residents may be less vulnerable than those with only a few, since the greater the number, the less disastrous may be the loss of one for those who stay. Some species, on the other hand, such as the coast live oak, create their own small habitats, and loss of these key species is disastrous for those that depend on them. In fact, we don't know all the interactions necessary for species' survival and by the time we do understand them, many may be degraded or destroyed.

I've found that as people become more familiar with interactions among plants and animals, they take more delight in the ones living in the mountains. Too, such people are more aware of how they can affect mountain plants and animals, and the mountains themselves. Awareness leads to improved safekeeping of the wild heart of Los Angeles and of other wild lands near burgeoning cities.

The network of interactions is complex, but some are obvious. One of the most familiar, and sometimes

Wasp parasites on variable checkerspot butterfly caterpillar, Mishe Mokwa Trail.

Sonoran bumblebee on Cleveland sage blossom.

dramatic, is consumption. Most people know that sunlight helps the chlorophyll of green plants turn chemical compounds into food. Plant-eaters consume this food and convert it into other proteins and energy, and meat-eaters absorb the proteins in animals, and turn much of the food into energy.

Many people (not myself) are more at ease with plant-eaters than meat-eaters, probably partly because, in the recent past, meat-eaters competed with people for high-quality food—or even ate people. A homeowner may be mildly upset when a mule deer browses his rosebuds, but horrified to see a mountain lion kill and eat the deer. I accept the goings-on of nature more readily.

If the homeowner finds a deer carcass after a lion has had its fill, he may see the cleanup crew in action: larvae of beetles and flies, vultures, or even domestic dogs. Other recyclers, like bacteria and fungi, are too small for him to see, though he may smell the results of their work. Such stinks don't offend me, because I know the recyclers turn leftovers into compounds they, and the rest of us, need to live.

The fuzzy white growths on the butterfly caterpillar in the photograph are cocoons of wasp larvae eating the caterpillar from the inside out. They repel me not only because they live at the expense of the host, like other parasites, but because they probably torture it.

People who specialize in insects call wasps like these "parasitoids." Unlike most parasites, they are large with respect to the host and eventually eat it up. This interaction straddles the border between consumption and parasitism.

Parasitism is another instance of a direct interaction between species. Some parasites, particularly among insects, are essential for keeping populations from exceeding the capacity of the ecosystem to support them.

In contrast, commensalism, a harmless interaction between species, can be rather charming. For example, California mice, one of our common wild mice, often live in dusky-footed woodrat nests, which shelter the mice from weather and predators. The mouse does not harm the woodrat, because the nests are quite spacious enough for many more tenants than the woodrat alone.

And mutualism, which benefits *both* of the parties to an interaction, can be truly beautiful. The flower of Cleveland sage in my garden has distinctive color, shape, and odor that attract bumblebees and guide them to the nectar and pollen for their offspring. The blossom produces these delights not to please me but to make sure bumblebees will pick up pollen to carry to another blossom, thereby helping the sage reproduce sexually. Most flowering plants have similar interactions with their pollinators.

Another interaction between species is mimicry. The hornet moth looks like a wasp and few birds would try to eat it (nor would I try to pick it up) though it is actually defenseless. The moth lives in the same habitat as the wasp and has evolved to wear its warning shape and color. Thus, the moth interacts indirectly with the wasp by mimicking it.

When a robin eats the fruits of holly-leaf cherry and defecates later, it plants cherry pits away from the parent shrub. This is just one instance of many in which one species interacts with a second by dispersing seeds, so individuals of the second species will

California mouse on chamise. (RS)

Pampas Grass choking out vegetation along Pacific Coast Highway.

Mountain lion warning, Los Liones trailhead.

have a better chance to grow because they do not compete with the parent for resources.

Sexual reproduction is an interaction between individuals of the same species. Later, I'll describe some of the more colorful and bizarre sexual escapades. There will be plenty of opportunities, because from spiders to mountain lions, from fungi to sunflowers, most organisms do it, at least part of the time.

But access to too few individuals may lead to inbreeding, birth defects, and deterioration of the remaining population. To ensure the survival of mountain lions, for instance, it is not enough to avoid killing them. They must have room to breed (100 square miles for a male competing with other males for a mate) as well as to live. Some mountain lions survive in the Santa Monicas, as the warning sign attests.

Camouflage illustrates an interaction between an organism and its environment. The color and pattern of rough tree bark on the forewings of the walnut underwing moth help it hide. If it's attacked anyway, the flash of the underwings often startles the predator into dropping it.

Hornet mimicking wasp. (CH)

Camouflaged underwing moth.

In many coastal areas, pampas grass creates spectacular fountains of green and ivory, completely filling lowlands and marching up canyons. This plant is native to Argentina, not California, and has escaped from people's gardens.

Without its natural controls, it, and especially its aggressive cousin, jubata grass, chokes out native plants, thereby creating an impenetrable mass that provides little natural food or shelter for wildlife. I've seen miles of it filling the disturbed roadside along the Pan American Highway in Costa Rica, where few birds sing and few animals live. As of 1995, many horticulturalists were recommending against landscaping with any species of pampas grass. Too late for the California coast?

I'll end this overview with a story of interactions among bats, people, the structure of the environment, insects, and plants. Some people dislike or fear bats and, I confess, their avid little faces once unsettled me. (I must have imagined what a monster a hyena-sized bat would be.) However, bats are valuable because they are the main predators of moths and other night-flying insects, many of which damage people's crops and gardens.

Bats need safe places to roost and breed, but permanent streams and, consequently, trees for bats to roost in, are scarce in the Santa Monicas. In the past, old wooden sheds and shacks made good bat roosts. Now, people are replacing the old buildings with more permanent structures, and, because the dispossessed bats have nowhere else to "hang out," their numbers are declining. To stop this decline, some people are putting up bat houses, but these will attract bats only if bats are already in nearby wild areas.

The ecosystems in the Santa Monica Mountains arise from their geography, their geologic and evolutionary history, their human history, their accessibility to people, and, most important, people's attitudes toward them.

Doubtless, for thousands of years, people have responded to our mountains with affection and respect, but the earliest descriptions I found were written nearly a century ago by Frederick Rindge. An educated, perceptive man, he traveled in Europe and the United States before settling on his Rancho Topanga-Malibu-Sequit (Fig. 1), which stretched along the coast from Topanga to Arroyo Sequit and extended from the sea to the crest of the range. Among his joys were the "dark green mountain chaparral jungles," the "mountainside glorified with the wild lilac in full blue bloom," and "these great bulwarks of strength, these mountains."

Legend has it that Padre Juan Crespi was responsible for the name of the mountains. On Saint Monica's feast day in June 1770, during Portola's trek north from San Diego, Crespi named a group of

Frederick Rindge. (SRAN)

Long-eared bat. (MP)

9

pools where he took a refreshing bath *Los Ojitos de Santa Monica.* In Spanish, *ojo* means eye, and *ojito,* small eye. Since *ojito* also means pool, the word seems to echo the romantic phrase: "your eyes are like pools." These pools were somewhere in the Los Angeles Basin, but exactly where we don't know.

It took me several years to get used to the orientation of the Santa Monica Mountains, because, being part of the Transverse Ranges, they run east and west, not north and south. I *still* have to remind myself that the Pacific Ocean is *south* of the Santa Monicas, *not* west.

Obvious geographical, geological, and ecological features set the Santa Monicas off from the other Transverse Ranges.

Main roads mark the boundaries. Rather than being mere artifacts, however, the roads follow natural discontinuities in southern California topography such as the Los Angeles River, which follows the break between the Santa Monicas and the western foothills of the San Gabriels.

At first, I was surprised to read in Crespi's log, written on August 4, 1769, that scouts, looking for a way north from their camp near the La Brea tar pits, had found:

> no way past the range falling steep to the sea; they say many high rough mountain ranges run along to northwestward and northward, but in one of those directions we shall have to go, however God may assist us in doing.

But Los Angeles's infatuation with the automobile has broached Crespi's formidable barrier and I can follow his routes on high-speed, eight-lane freeways through Sepulveda Pass, Cahuenga Pass, and the Los Angeles River Valley, which became part of *El Camino Real,* the King's Highway.

By this date, highways enclose the undeveloped land that native animals need to reproduce. Although foothills of the mountains spill beyond the highways into the Los Angeles Basin and San Fernando Valley, these areas are too urbanized for animals such as mule deer, mountain lion, red-tailed hawk and quail to breed there, though they visit occasionally or even frequently.

Figure 3 shows the Pacific Coast Highway running along the southern edge of the mountains beside the Pacific Ocean. Here, the mountains thrust directly from the sea to form a coastline of sandy and stony beaches, coastal terraces, steep canyons, and rocky crests that reveal the bones of the land.

Near Point Mugu, the mountains continue beneath the ocean to pop up as the Northern Channel Islands. There is evidence, however, that ocean has separated the islands from the mainland for at least 17,000 years, and they have been too far from the mainland for some animals to colonize them. (For example, they have no coyotes.) Because island animals and plants differ from those on the mainland in this and many other ways, I do not include them.

Near Calleguas (pronounced *ka-yéa-was*) Creek and Conejo (pronounced *ko-néa-ho*) Creek, the western end of the mountains rises out of the Oxnard Plain. In the mid-1950s, the Ventura Freeway began to slice toward the plain through the northern edge of the mountains. This freeway became the first of a series of hurdles for wildlife, trying to move among the Santa Monica Mountains, the other Transverse Ranges to the east, and the Coast Ranges to the north.

Relative to their surroundings—the Pacific Ocean, the Los Angeles Basin, and the San Fernando Valley—the Santa Monicas are small and vulnerable.

The length of the range, 46 miles from Griffith Park to Point Mugu, is substantial, but it averages only 7.5 miles wide. At the eastern end, alien plants and animals have invaded all of Griffith Park.

From the mouth of Santa Monica Canyon to Point Mugu, rocky cliffs thrust above a glistening coastal strand and waves thump and sigh on a sandy or pebbled shore. Here, also, remain two of the few, large wetlands in southern California: Malibu Lagoon and Mugu Lagoon. A rich melange of inter-tidal animals crowds both areas and, from September through May, they host large flocks of migrating and wintering water birds.

The mountains rise from the ocean for 35 miles, but the effects of the sea are far more profound than this short stretch might suggest, since the ocean shapes the climate of the mountains and the coast. The coastal climate is moderate, which encourages the continued growth of population around Los Angeles. In addition, tangy ocean breezes and sunny beaches have drawn people in search of a relaxing, healthful life and have created southern California's cult of the fit, trim body. More profoundly, the effects of the ocean on the climate of the Santa Monica Mountains have influenced the evolution of plants and animals native to the range.

In the past, the ocean supported a diverse group of marine animals—fish, seals and sea lions, whales, dolphins, sea otters, and sea birds—and an easily accessible intertidal zone, teeming with crabs, clams, sea snails, and other tasty morsels, that supplied California Indians with food and clothing for at least 10,000 years. Though the sea otters are gone and only remnants of the fur seals remain, harbor seals, sea lions, and fish are still plentiful, and the swirling, calling flocks of sea birds still enhance the beauty of the strand.

Since the early 1900s, people living around the mountains have viewed them as a retreat from the city—even a defense against it. In the 1920s, when people started pouring into the Los Angeles Basin, along with the water that William Mulholland's aqueduct siphoned from the Sierra Nevadas, building in the mountains began in earnest.

Today people continue to escape the city by stacking home sites up the mountain slopes. As roads and houses climb the steep hillsides, they squeeze native flora and fauna into ever-diminishing areas. At the same time, people encourage the expansion of species that flourish alongside people—the northern mockingbird, cabbage butterfly, and castor bean, to name a few.

Malibu Lagoon.

The Los Angeles Basin is, very roughly, a square, 30 miles on each side; it lies between the Pacific Ocean on the west and south, the Santa Ana Mountains on the east, and the Transverse Ranges on the north.

In 1769 the basin was a shrubby, grassy plain with flowing rivers (in mid-summer, the Los Angeles and San Gabriel rivers and the Rio Hondo carried fresh, pure water), lush, green river valleys and fresh-water springs. Parts of the basin were marshy, giving rise to the use of the Spanish word, *cienega*, which means marsh, and is found in the names of some of the Mexican ranchos near the Los Angeles River. Winter and spring floods destroyed several early Spanish settlements and led to the first flood control works, which have profoundly affected the basin and the

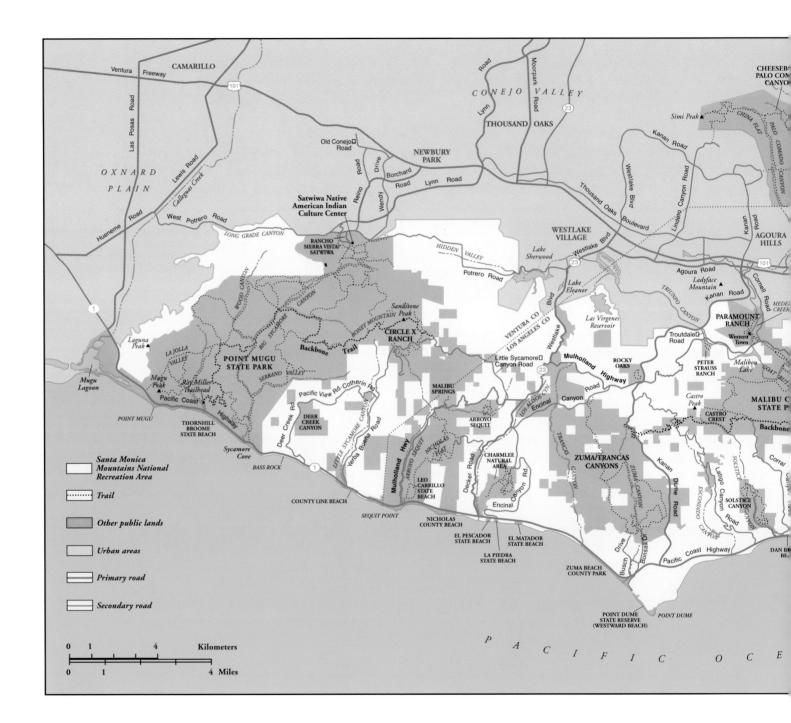

Santa Monica
Mountains National
Recreation Area

Trail

Other public lands

Urban areas

Primary road

Secondary road

0 1 4 Kilometers

0 1 4 Miles

CAMARILLO

CHEESEBC
PALO CO
CANYON

CONEJO VALLEY

THOUSAND OAKS

OXNARD PLAIN

Ventura Freeway

Las Posas Road

Lewis Road

Hueneme Road

West Potrero Road

Calleguas Creek

Old Conejo Road

NEWBURY PARK

Borchard Road

Lynn Road

Reino Road

Wendy Drive

Moorpark Road

Lynn Road

Road

Thousand Oaks Blvd

Simi Peak

CHINA FLAT

PALO COMADO CANYON

Satwiwa Native
American Indian
Culture Center

RANCHO SIERRA VISTA/
SATWIWA

LONG GRADE CANYON

HIDDEN VALLEY

Potrero Road

Lake Sherwood

WESTLAKE VILLAGE

Westlake Blvd

Agoura Road

AGOURA HILLS

Lindero Canyon Road

Cornell Road

MEDEA CREEK

WOOD CANYON

BIG SYCAMORE CANYON

Sandstone Peak

HONEY MOUNTAIN TRAIL

CIRCLE X RANCH

Lake Eleanor

Las Virgenes Reservoir

Ladyface Mountain

TRIUNFO CANYON

Kanan Road

PARAMOUNT RANCH

Laguna Peak

LA JOLLA VALLEY

POINT MUGU STATE PARK

Backbone Trail

SERRANO VALLEY

Troutdale Road

Little Sycamore Canyon Road

Mulholland Highway

ROCKY OAKS

Western Town

PETER STRAUSS RANCH

Malibou Lake

Castro Peak

MALIBU STATE PA

Mugu Lagoon

Mugu Peak

Ray Miller Trailhead

Pacific Coast Highway

POINT MUGU

THORNHILL BROOME STATE BEACH

Deer Creek Rd

DEER CREEK CANYON

Pacific View Rd

Cotherin Rd

LITTLE SYCAMORE CANYON

Yerba Buena Road

MALIBU SPRINGS

ARROYO SEQUIT

VENTURA CO.

LOS ANGELES CO.

LOS ALISOS CYN

Westlake Blvd

Encinal Canyon Road

CASTRO CREST

Backbone

Sycamore Cove

BASS ROCK

Mulholland Hwy

ARROYO SEQUIT

NICHOLAS FLAT

CHARMLEE NATURAL AREA

TRANCAS CANYON

ZUMA/TRANCAS CANYONS

Kanan Dune Road

SOLSTICE CANYON

ESCONDIDO CANYON

GOAT BUTTE

COUNTY LINE BEACH

SEQUIT POINT

LEO CARRILLO STATE BEACH

Decker Road

Encinal

ZUMA CANYON

Latigo Canyon Road

Corral

NICHOLAS COUNTY BEACH

EL PESCADOR STATE BEACH

EL MATADOR STATE BEACH

LA PIEDRA STATE BEACH

ZUMA BEACH COUNTY PARK

Busch Dr

Bonsall Dr

Pacific Coast Highway

DAN BL
BEA

POINT DUME STATE RESERVE (WESTWARD BEACH)

POINT DUME

PACIFIC OCE

Figure 3: Boundaries of Santa Monica Mountains, roads, parks, and preserves.

Toyon (California holly) in bloom in Santa Ynez Canyon.

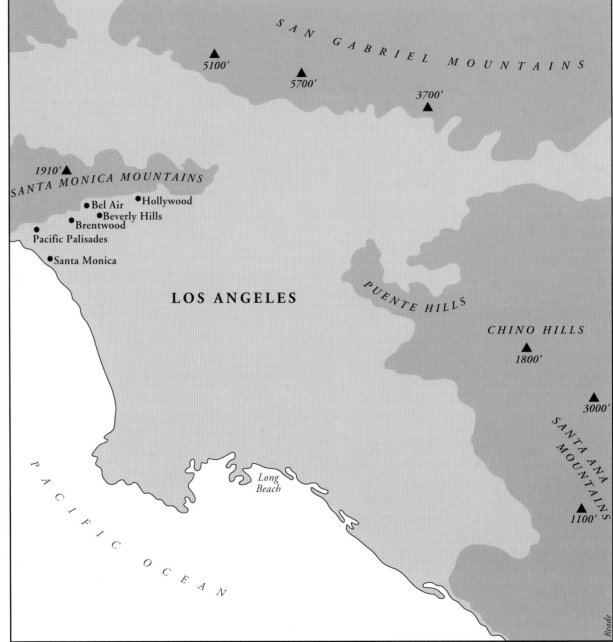

Figure 4: The Los Angeles Basin.

mountains.

A hundred years later, European settlers used the basin largely for ranching and growing Mediterranean crops, such as olives, citrus, and grapes. They installed drains to control the floods that poured out of the mountains in winter and to make more land suitable for agriculture, and shot or drove out all but a remnant of the grizzly bears.

By that time, too, the culture of the Gabrielinos and Fernandeños was well on its way to extinction. *Gabrielino* is the name the Spanish gave to the California Indians who lived within kidnaping distance of the San Gabriel Mission and they called those close to the San Fernando Mission "Fernandeños."

Today, the Los Angeles Basin contains many independent communities, along with dozens of suburbs within the City of Los Angeles. Because of the entertainment industry, several of the communities that border the mountains are known the world over.

Near their east end is Hollywood, which schoolchildren learn is named for the California holly, a native shrub growing profusely in the range. The Spanish called it *toyon*, and its clusters of bright red berries appear in December, giving it yet another name, "Christmas berry."

Going west along the southern slopes of the mountains, movie stars and wealthy people have made their homes in Beverly Hills and Bel Air. Next come Pacific Palisades, Topanga, and Malibu, clambering the mountain slopes above the sea. From several points along this coast, I have enjoyed one of the incongruities of Los Angeles: watching the sun *rise* over the Pacific Ocean.

The names of these communities reflect their diverse history. Some are from names the California Indians used for their villages. Malibu comes from the Chumash *humaliwo,* meaning "the surf sounds loudly," and Mugu from the Chumash *muwu,* "hand of the beach."

The Chumash are the California Indians living northwest of the mountains. They applied *muwu* to Mugu Lagoon, and, indeed, sandspits reach like fingers across the mouth of Calleguas Creek. As far as is known, Malibu was the easternmost Chumash village.

The meaning of "Topanga," from the Gabrielino *topaa'nga,* as well as the location of the Gabrielino area of the same name, have both been lost. It is commonly (but inaccurately) said that Topanga means "where the mountains meet the sea."

The San Fernando Valley borders the mountains on the north. Padre Crespi's first view of the valley was of "a very large valley all burnt off by the heathens, that from the height looked to have been all fallowed" (i.e., left dormant after plowing). As the Spanish proceeded, he noted that the valley was "all very good, very grassy soil, though most of it had been burnt off."

Hillside development in Santa Ynez Canyon.

That California Indians burned the land did not surprise the Spanish. Even today people like the *campesenos* (farmers in Latin America), who depend on wild vegetation for part of their livelihood, set fire to dry summer grasses to encourage new growth and return nutrients to the soil.

Until World War II, the San Fernando Valley held oak woodlands, grassland, scrub, orchards,

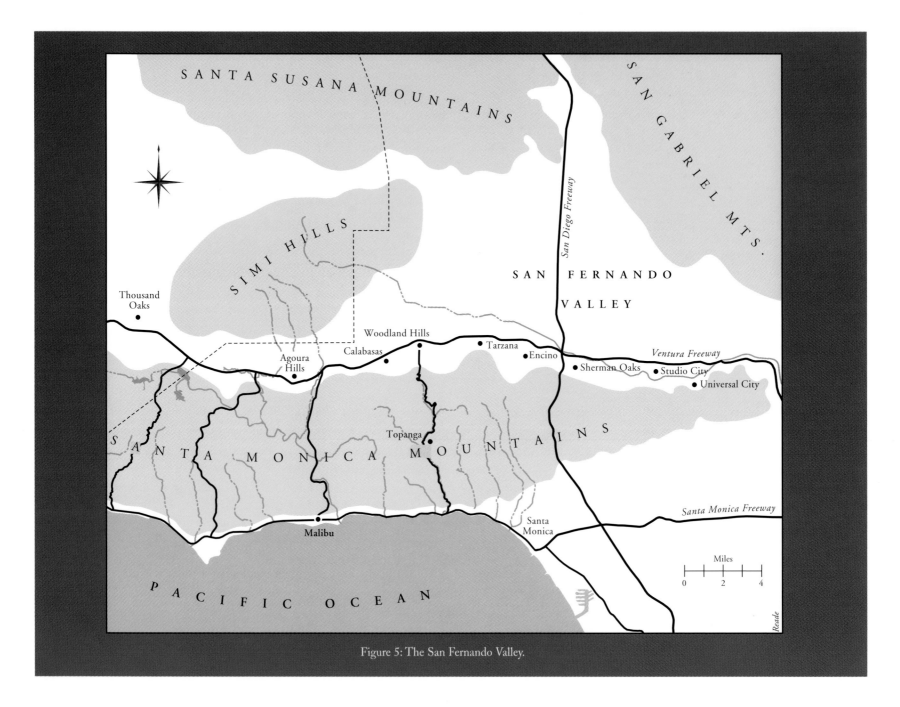

Figure 5: The San Fernando Valley.

farms, and ranches. With the explosion of population after the war, development of the north slopes of the mountains intensified. Now, for nearly 40 miles, small communities blend into each other from east to west, along the Ventura Freeway, before it spills down to the Oxnard Plain.

The names of some of these communities evoke the landscape and the mighty oaks that dominated it before Europeans arrived: Sherman Oaks, Woodland Hills, Thousand Oaks, and Encino. Many of the oaks were the valley oak, which formed groves of majestic trees, heedlessly reduced to a pathetic few during the early days of expansion. In the summer of 1769, the Portola expedition named the plain around Encino the "Valley of Santa Catalina de Bononia de los Encinos" for the many coast live oaks growing there. Though we now call this area the San Fernando Valley, the name of Encino lingers to commemorate these beautiful trees.

On the other hand, Calabasas gets its name from the Spanish *calabaza,* which means "squash" or "pumpkin." Perhaps at this spot pumpkins saved the Spanish settlers from starvation, but I've found no record of that dramatic derivation.

The names of Universal City and Studio City reflect the movie industry, and Tarzana was named to honor Edgar Rice Burroughs, who wrote the *Tarzan* books, lived in Tarzana, and is buried there.

Little distinguishes one of these suburbs from the next. They are mostly middle-class communities that become newer from east to west; only forty years ago people who lived in Calabasas seemed like modern pioneers.

When traffic is flowing smoothly, the freeways let me bypass the Santa Monicas at speeds well above the posted maximum. Because freeways limit my ability to get on or off, I usually use what Angelenos call "surface streets" to enter the mountains. Figure 3 shows some of the major roads: Mulholland Drive, the Pacific Coast Highway, Topanga Canyon Boulevard, and Malibu Canyon Boulevard.

In 1925, Mulholland Drive was officially opened with much fanfare, culminated by a "celebration in the Hollywood Bowl with a galaxy of movie stars showered with roses from a fleet of airplanes." The new road honored William Mulholland, who engineered and oversaw the construction of the Los Angeles Aqueduct, one of the few massive projects in California that was completed within budget and on schedule.

As shown on Figure 3, Mulholland Drive starts at the west end of a bridge over the Hollywood Freeway connecting the east and west sides of Cahuenga Pass. In addition to automobiles, some of my friends see deer and coyotes use the bridge. From its west end, at which the road is about 11 miles northeast of the coast and a thousand feet in elevation, Mulholland wiggles its way up the northwest side of the pass into the Hollywood Hills.

For roughly 30 miles, the road winds around the crest of the mountains. Along the way are stunning vistas of the San Fernando Valley or the Los Angeles Basin, and one of the organizations devoted to preserving the mountains for the public maintains areas where I often park to savor the view. The sights are especially spectacular after dark, because, in comparison with the cities of the East and Midwest, few tall trees hide the glitter of lights flung across hundreds of square miles below.

The road also provides sweeping views of the chaparral-covered mountains, and several trail heads encourage me to park and hike into the wilderness. In

Valley Oak in Malibu Creek State Park.

many places, road-cuts have exposed steep walls of rock that tell geological history, and, at a number of these sites, people often putter about looking for fossils.

Except for a 10-mile stretch of rough, dirt road between the San Diego Freeway and near Topanga Canyon Boulevard, Mulholland is paved. Pavement has encouraged residential development and consequent depletion of wild land. So far, however, conservation groups have blocked efforts to pave the dirt portion and forestalled the bulldozers that precede

home construction.

I challenge you to stay on Mulholland after its intersection with Decker Canyon Road. If you get lost, you may end up near Sandstone Peak from which the views are spectacular. If you stay on Mulholland, you'll find it dips south through the mountains, along the deep canyon of the Arroyo Sequit, and reaches the ocean at the Pacific Coast Highway. The state and federal governments have set aside much of the steep hillsides in Arroyo Sequit Canyon and above Leo Carrillo Beach for

Coast live oak in Malibu Creek State Park.

People digging fossils in old Topanga Canyon.

public enjoyment.

Roughly parallel to Mulholland Drive, the Pacific Coast Highway borders the southern edge of the Santa Monica Mountains from Santa Monica to Point Mugu. Rindge began the fight against the Pacific Coast Highway in 1894, when he installed, and locked, gates on the wagon road to Santa Barbara that went through his Malibu rancho. His widow, hoping to protect her idyllic treasure from the public onslaught she knew would come if the road were opened, continued the battle for more than a quarter of a century. In 1925 she was defeated by a U.S. Supreme Court decision granting the State of California a road easement through her ranch.

These days, when the Pacific Coast Highway, familiarly known as PCH, is closed to through traffic, it is usually because rocks and mud have slid down the steep bluffs and blocked the road. When that happens, old-time residents honor the memory of the rancho by saying, "There goes Rindge's Revenge."

I do not often think of the Rindges when I am driving on PCH below the bluffs of my mountain

View to northeast from Sandstone Peak.

range. Instead, I chafe at the houses perched above the beach that limit my view of the ocean to quick snatches. The beach houses thin out after Encinal Canyon Road, and, from there to Point Mugu, I often imagine I'm a seabird soaring beside the breaking waves.

High bluffs and steep hills crowd the north side of the road. (Remember, PCH runs east and west.) West of Zuma Beach, in the springtime, giant coreopsis splash bouquets of luminous yellow on the cliffs, and, later, tall, white yucca blooms punctuate the dark green hillsides like candles. The open land tempts me to leave the highway, on one of the more than a dozen roads winding up the canyons toward the crest of the range.

One of these, Big Sycamore Canyon, carves its way through Point Mugu State Park to Hidden Valley, at the northern border of the range. As of 1989, this enormous park enclosed some 15,000 acres of wild land, with rocky peaks and ridges, mountain lions, and golden eagles.

Returning to the central part of the range, Topanga Canyon Boulevard reaches Mulholland Highway about 12 miles from PCH. For most of this stretch, the road curves so sharply and so often, I just take my time to enjoy the beautiful, wooded canyon through which I'm passing. In winter, red toyon berries spark the dark green of the chaparral, and, in spring, flowering branches of wild lilac spill pale blue and white down the banks and over the road.

About 6 miles up the road is the village of Topanga, which, despite the continuing efforts of the residents, is losing its rural atmosphere. When driving through the village at night, I take special care because people and dogs often wander onto the highway.

The entrance to the headquarters of Topanga

Landslide on Pacific Coast Highway. (PM)

Giant coreopsis in bloom.

State Park is off Entrada Road just north of the village center. In 1985, this 9,000-acre park, another jewel of the state park system, contained 32 miles of trails through stream side vegetation, oak woodland, grassland, and chaparral.

Topanga Canyon Boulevard breaks out from woods and chaparral at the crest of the range, 1,500 feet in elevation at this point. One can overlook the entire San Fernando Valley to the north, but miles of chaparral-covered ridges block the sight of the ocean to the south. From the crest, Topanga Creek flows south for about 7 miles before it reaches the ocean, whereas its north-flowing counterpart reaches the San Fernando Valley in less than a mile.

Moving west along PCH, the next major route into the mountains is Malibu Canyon Boulevard. For

View of Malibu Canyon.

View of Topanga Canyon.

some 3 miles after entering, the road clings to the western wall of the canyon, 300 to 400 feet above the creek, and offers some of the most breathtaking views in southern California. As I follow the bends of the creek bed below, the rugged eastern face of the canyon wheels before me, sometimes rising 500 feet above the road. Just before the last sharp bend to the north, the ridge is higher than 1,500 feet.

The canyon walls, sometimes steeper than 45 degrees, hold sparse vegetation and reveal strata of tan, mauve, dark brown, and beige, tilted at absurd angles. The panorama exposes the violence creating the mountains through which the creek carves its path.

Past Tapia Park, most of the kinks and curls in the road disappear, and, for nearly 2 miles, I have easy going on the tree-lined road through rural countryside, to the entrance to Malibu Creek State Park. As of 1989, this 7,000-acre park included preserves of valley oak, golden eagle nesting areas, and rare plants; sites of historic adobes and ranch houses; and Malibu Lagoon.

Malibu Canyon Boulevard intersects Mulholland Highway just beyond the park entrance. The stretch of road north of Mulholland is called Las Virgenes Road, a name Portola gave a Chumash village where he camped in August 1769. The chief had three virgin daughters, which so impressed Portola that he named his campsite "Las Virgenes."

Just beyond the intersection with Mulholland, another Los Angeles incongruity appears among the trees on the east, and disappears just as suddenly—a frosted, elaborate Hindu temple.

The Santa Monica Mountains are an island of wild land surrounded by seas of people. More than three million live near and in them, more than twelve million within an hour's drive. That closeness is both the marvel of the mountains and the threat to their wild freedom.

Even before the surge in Los Angeles's population in the 1920s, many people understood that the Santa Monica Mountains had more to offer than pedestals for houses. The athletic can run, hike, climb, surf, swim, bicycle, or ride horseback in an atmosphere sea breezes have washed clean of pollution. Others can drive along mountain roads, sunbathe, picnic, fish, bird-watch, or study other aspects of nature. And trails are available so handicapped people can enjoy the out-of-doors. The beauty of the Santa Monica Mountains makes each of these experiences special.

The range is also a laboratory for biological research at the many, world-renowned institutions nearby—the Museums of Natural History of Los Angeles and Santa Barbara, the Los Angeles and Santa Barbara campuses of the University of California, Pepperdine University, and other universities and colleges.

The only way to ensure that the Santa Monica Mountains will continue to serve not only homebuilders, but the world at large, is to protect a significant portion of the range from development. Colonel Griffith was the first to set land in the Santa Monica Mountains aside for the general public in 1896, when he gave an area he had been using for an ostrich farm to Los Angeles. (Angelenos enjoy the exotic.) Figure 3 shows Griffith Park as well as other parks in the range. East of Cahuenga Pass, Griffith Park contains more than 4,000 acres, much of it still home to deer and coyote, and is the largest city-owned park in the United States.

The movement to preserve the mountains took off in earnest in 1971, when Sierra Club members marched down Mulholland Drive to "Save the Santa Monicas." In 1978, Congress established the Santa Monica Mountains National Recreation Area to:

> preserve and enhance its scenic, natural, and historical setting and its public health value as an airshed for the Southern California metropolitan area while providing for the recreational and educational needs of the visiting public.

At that time, the boundary of the National Recreation Area (Figure 3), encompassed 150,000 acres, of which 75,000 acres were planned, as of 1995, eventually to be in public ownership. Even these will not sustain the natural vigor of their plants and animals, unless people understand and care for the mountains and their wildlife.

For me, and many others, the mountains offer both an escape from the crowding and pressures of urban life, and a chance to become absorbed in a wholly different kind of experience. People working together can ensure that those who follow us will be able to enjoy these experiences for the foreseeable future.

To emphasize its ecological focus, I've organized this book around a set of natural and man-made ecosystems, chosen to strike a balance between completeness and practicality. These are chaparral, sage-scrub, oak woodland and valley oak savanna, grassland, streams and stream sides, areas with quiet fresh water (pools, lakes, and marshes), areas with quiet salt water (marshes and marine meadows), coastal strand, and the tidal zone.

Ridges, canyons, streams and seeps, grassy patches, rocky outcrops, changes in elevation, and the like can interrupt each ecosystem. Rarely does one spread continuously over an area larger than a square mile. Thus, ecosystems form a patchwork quilt over the range.

The areas between the patches often belong to no clearly defined ecosystem. An area between chaparral and sage-scrub may contain both chamise, a common chaparral shrub, and buckwheat, frequent in sage-scrub. Such an area, where plants and animals characteristic of each ecosystem mingle, usually has more species than either ecosystem by itself.

People have created other ecosystems: vacant lots; roads and roadsides; planted fields and orchards; livestock farms; gardens and nurseries; parks, golf courses, and cemeteries; and the interiors and exteriors of buildings and houses. These have their own plants and animals and can affect the plants and animals of wild ecosystems nearby. For example, deer move into the suburbs because gardens supply food and water during the dry season.

People will continue to develop ecosystems in the Santa Monica Mountains for the foreseeable future. For the health of the native plants and animals people love, they must understand how man-made ecosystems affect wild ones and try to ensure that these effects promote the well-being of native species.

Hindu temple next to Malibu Canyon Road.

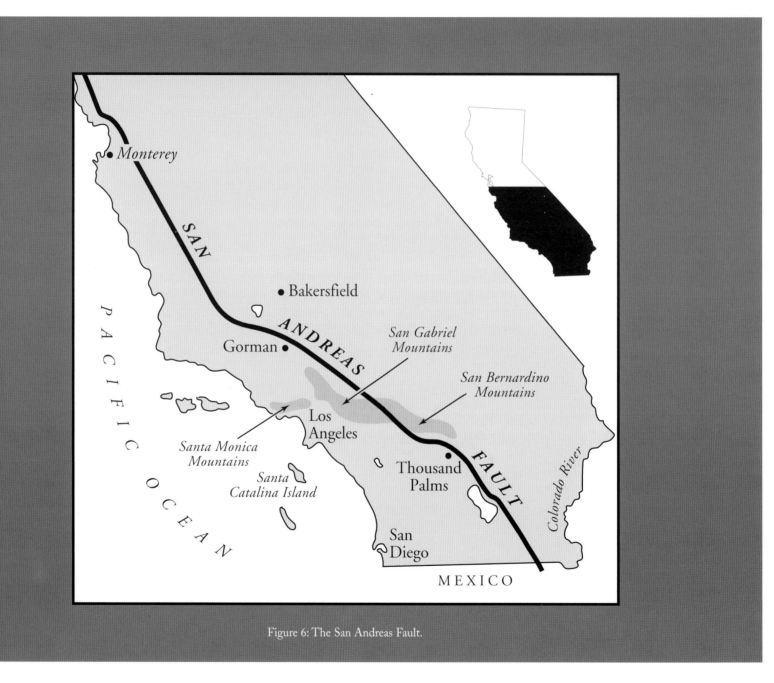

Figure 6: The San Andreas Fault.

CHAPTER 2

Creating the Range

SHAKING WOKE ME AT *4:31 A.M., JANUARY 17, 1994. "HERE WE GO AGAIN!" I SAID,* groping for the flashlight on the bed table. "My Mountains will have their way."

I was lucky. My family and home rode out the quake intact, but many others did not, and, in some places, our mountains grew a third of a foot.

If I had been a Chumash, I would have thought the two giant serpents, holding up the world, had moved. If I had been one of Portola's party, I would have thought volcanos were erupting in the Santa Monica Mountains.

Sliding, twisting, heaving, and sinking of the earth are building the Santa Monica Mountains; heavy rains and floods are sculpting the mountains as they rise. With sun, fog, wind, and fire, these forces create the ecosystems within which native plants and animals have evolved and within which we live today.

The movement of the Pacific Tectonic Plate past the North American Tectonic Plate powers these convulsions. Part of the boundary between the two plates is the notorious San Andreas Fault, on each side of which the land is sliding horizontally with respect to the land on the other side.

The map of the San Andreas (Figure 6) shows the present trend of this movement, which, within the past thirty million years, has taken the Pacific Plate some 870 miles northwest with respect to the North American Plate.

Los Angeles is more than 50 miles from the fault and the edge of the Pacific Plate. Thus, dire predictions notwithstanding, Los Angeles will not fall into the sea even when "The Big One" shakes southern California. But, though any of the several major thrust-faults under Los Angeles may cause a destructive quake, one caused by slippage along the San Andreas could be many times stronger.

The San Andreas is somehow involved with the unusual east-west trend of the Transverse Ranges. Beginning about thirty million years ago, the Pacific Plate began sliding along a new boundary with the North American Plate, causing the earth's crust to rotate clockwise up to 90 degrees in some places. That change makes the Pacific Plate butt into most of

Layers of twisted rock along Mulholland Highway.

Oak woodland in Topanga State Park.

assaults of winter rains and floods that, in older mountains, would have rounded off the crest and filled the canyon bottoms with soil.

Compression has deformed rocks so severely that, at several sites, it has completely overturned deposits around two million years old. In many locations the layers tilt almost 90 degrees from their original horizontal position or may be folded and twisted like taffy.

A road-cut on Mulholland Drive 1.5 miles west of the intersection with Las Virgenes Road has uncovered a dramatic example of contorted rock. The folding and twisting are so severe, geologists believe they may have occurred while the rock was still soft enough to deform in a short time without breaking.

The Santa Monica Mountains are very young, as mountains go, and, as Angelenos are all too aware, still suffer growing pains. The current uplift is only five million years old. Because of its relative youth, thin, rocky or gravelly soils cover much of the range. Their prevalence partly accounts for the extensive cover of shrubby plants. The rocks that comprise the range, however, formed during a series of sinkings and risings long before the current period of growth; some rocks are as old as 200 million years.

The east-west orientation of the Santa Monica Mountains profoundly affects the plants and animals that live here because it divides the mountains into mostly north-facing and mostly south-facing slopes. In North America, south-facing slopes get more intense sunlight for longer periods, both during the day and over the course of a year, than do north-facing slopes.

Very different ecosystems normally occur on the differently oriented slopes. On many north-facing slopes, I can stroll in cool shade under the massive

California while it slides by, compressing the land all along the San Andreas and creating the lattice of faults (some of which have yet to be discovered) that riddle southern California today. Compression has squeezed the Los Angeles Basin so much that Laguna Beach and Pasadena are 14 miles closer together than they were 2.2 million years ago.

Returning to Figure 6, we see that north of Gorman and south of Thousand Palms the San Andreas runs northwesterly, whereas in between, it runs west by northwesterly. In other words, the San Andreas makes a dogleg between these points.

All along the dogleg, compression is especially strong and is pushing up the Transverse Ranges at rates estimated to average 24 feet in a thousand years. The continuing uplift more than makes up for the

Chaparral with big pod ceanothus in bloom in Los Liones Canyon.

View south from Sandstone Peak.

boughs of coast live oaks, full of noisy, clown-faced acorn woodpeckers. On the other hand, I cannot penetrate the thick brush on most south-facing slopes, but must stick to existing trails, beside which California thrashers scramble for insects under chaparral shrubs.

More than half of the central and eastern part of the range faces south. Figure 7 shows Sepulveda Canyon in profile as an example. From the Santa Monica Freeway in the Los Angeles Basin, this canyon takes about 8 miles to rise to the crest, near Mulholland, and my car easily maintains a pace of 65 miles an hour. Going over the pass from the San Fernando Valley side is another matter. The road reaches the crest from the Ventura Freeway in about 2 miles, and I have to tread on the accelerator to keep up my speed while many other vehicles fall behind.

Uplifting of the land along local faults, and heavier erosion on slopes that face the ocean, have created the offset of the crest and the steeper slopes on the north side. Also, the eastern part of the San Fernando Valley is 600 feet higher than the Los Angeles Basin, as shown on Figure 7, which adds to the offset of the crest.

In the western portion of the range, south-facing slopes do not predominate because a different set of faults underlies it. In addition, between fourteen and sixteen million years ago volcanos baked or spewed out most of the igneous rocks underlying this portion, and these rocks do not crumble and slide as easily as do those in the eastern portion.

The Santa Monica Mountains are only moderately high, with an average elevation around 1,000 feet. They reach their highest point, 3,111 feet, at Sandstone Peak on the eastern end of the ridge of Boney Mountain.

Atop Sandstone Peak, I have looked over the ocean to the south and west and seen the Channel Islands piercing the water like the mountain peaks they are. My view has stretched from Catalina to Santa Cruz and, on a clear day, even included San Nicolas, more than 65 miles away. To the northwest I have seen the Oxnard Plain bordered by the ridges of the Santa Ynez and Topatopa Mountains. Rocky peaks and chaparral-covered ridges and canyons stretch out of sight to the north and east.

Several peaks along the ridge of Boney Mountain are nearly as high as Sandstone. Although the ridge is the color of sandstone, it is of volcanic origin. Volcanic deposits from the north overthrust older rock layers, making ridges separated by high valleys.

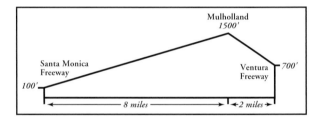

Figure 7: Profile of Sepulveda Pass (not to scale).

Some of these, such as Hidden Valley and Potrero Valley, hang on the northern mountain slopes above the Ventura Freeway.

Except in the western part, most of the surface rocks are sedimentary. Sedimentary rocks are composed of fine particles of preexisting rock that settled onto the floor of the ocean or, sometimes, in lakes or at the mouths of rivers. As time passed, the weight of overlying sediments squeezed those beneath into stone. Obvious layers characterize most of these surface rocks, which formed between six and twenty-five

Layered rock on Calabasas Peak.

View of Boney Mountain from Yerba Buena Road.

million years ago.

For example, from several points along Stunt Road one can see Calabasas Peak, made of layers of sandstone about twenty million years old. The peak is so full of marine fossils, we call the trail leading to it "Fossil Ridge."

Along Old Topanga Canyon Road, 1.2 miles south of Mulholland, a large, crumbling cliff contains a well-known collection of fossils. Here, people have found remains of more than a hundred species of clams, snails, and other invertebrates, as well as whales and sharks. Occasionally someone finds a fossil ammonite, a shellfish extinct for more than a hundred million years.

Some these fossils are so soft that when I tried to wash one, parts of it began to dissolve. Thus it is not surprising that even during the dry season, many of these rocks disintegrate and fall down the cliffs and hillsides.

All through the north side of the range, rock layers dip 12 to 15 degrees toward the San Fernando Valley and during heavy rains, slide toward the valley

Slide area along Pacific Coast Highway.

Ammonite fossil found along Mulholland Highway.

floor. Landslides—scarps, slumps, rock falls, rock flows, and every other example of mass wasting—form the most widespread surface feature in the range. The clays between the rock layers often leach out and grease the skids as the rocks tumble down.

The foot of the resulting landslide may be an aggregation of heavy, clay soil that holds so much water during the rainy season, that only grasses can live in it. Most southern California shrubs drown or rot in water-logged soil. Later in the year, the soil becomes a dry, rocklike mass in which trees, which need year-round ground water, cannot survive. This is why geologists look for hummocky, grassy patches as indicators of previous landslides.

Heavy rain and winter flooding have scoured deep canyons running south from the crest of the mountains to the sea or the Los Angeles Basin. More than twenty stream-cut canyons lie between Franklin

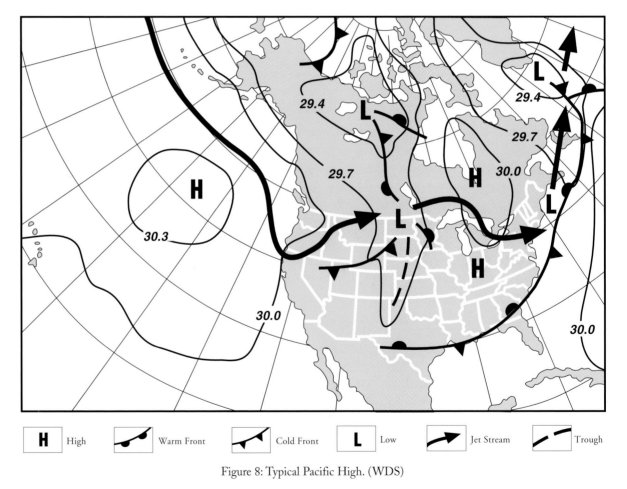

| **H** | High | Warm Front | Cold Front | **L** | Low | Jet Stream | Trough |

Figure 8: Typical Pacific High. (WDS)

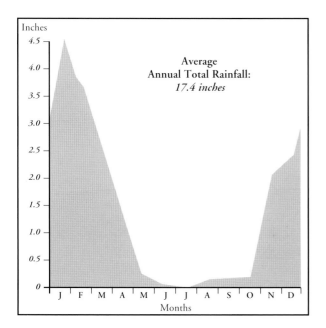

Average
Annual Total Rainfall:
17.4 inches

Figure 9: Rainfall by month at low elevations.

and Sycamore Canyons.

Southern California has hot, dry summers and cool (but not cold), wet winters. The Pacific High, a semipermanent, high-pressure air mass over the eastern North Pacific Ocean, primarily determines the weather. Figure 8 is a weather map showing a Pacific High. Air moves clockwise around it between 30 and 40 degrees North Latitude. Humid, tropical trade winds blow south of it; storms from the west move north of it.

Air usually moves from west to east over southern California. Before the air arrives, the Pacific High has compressed it, making it dry, warm, and stable. During the summer and early fall, the High generally deflects approaching westerly storms, so they cross over the Pacific Northwest. Under the subtropical sun, southern California bakes for months on end.

Perhaps the relentless assault of the sun is what caused the Chumash to see the sun as the Agent of Death and assign to Him the task of carrying off the dead to the world above.

Almost all rain falls between November and April. Figure 9 shows average rainfall by month from data gathered at the University of California at Los Angeles (UCLA), during a fifty-year period. UCLA lies at the base of the Santa Monica Mountains, and monthly rainfall there typifies rainfall patterns in the mountains at low elevations.

Over millions of years, plants and animals have evolved various strategies to survive during the annual, six-month drought. Some plants drop their leaves to conserve moisture; some animals sleep the summer away in burrows. But with plenty of water coming from the tap, I can revel in being outdoors during the months of sunshine.

During late fall through spring, the Pacific High sometimes weakens and shifts southward or westward, and a low-pressure trough forms over the western U.S. This lets the large-scale storms that gather over the Gulf of Alaska dip southward and bring moist, unstable air to our area. These storms follow the prevailing air flow southward, along the coast.

Once the Pacific High has shifted, it may stay that way for a week or more or may shift several times in succession, letting one storm after another enter southern California within a few days. Most of the rain in the Santa Monica Mountains arrives in storm patterns like this, and practically all precipitation in the mountains is rain.

When rain has been falling for several days, the ground becomes saturated, and flows of mud and gravel can sweep trees and boulders (and sometimes houses) down hillsides and cliffs. The debris may end

View of San Nicholas Canyon from Nicholas Flat.

Fallen house along Pacific Coast Highway.

Houses along Pacific Coast Highway with undercut patios.

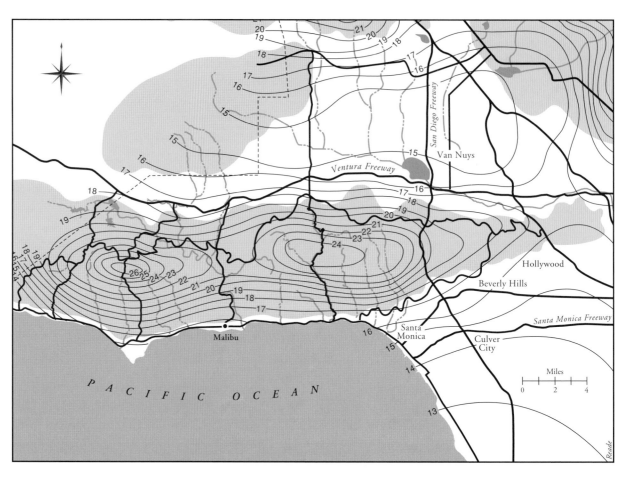

Figure 10: Contours of average annual rainfall in inches in the Santa Monica Mountains.

up in basins at the foot of rushing rivers, on roads already awash, or in houses. Visitors are amazed when I show them houses along PCH with decks cantilevered over a sheer, 200-foot drop. The earthquake of 1994 toppled one of these houses down the bluff.

When air moves in from the west, the mountains force it up, and its temperature falls. As temperature drops, the capacity of the air for holding water vapor

drops, too, and the air releases the water vapor as rain. In this way, the mountains increase rainfall on their south-facing slopes and may even produce it when none occurs at lower elevations.

Because most of the rain comes with winter storms moving in from the Pacific, slopes facing the sea are rainier than those facing inland. Figure 10 illustrates these effects. Note that average annual rainfall varies from about 15 inches at Point Dume and in the San Fernando Valley to almost twice as much (more than 26 inches) near Castro Peak, which is 2,824 feet high.

Not only does rainfall vary widely from place-to-place and month-to-month, but total rainfall varies widely from year-to-year, as shown by rain data for Topanga in Figure 11. Topanga is on the seaward side of Saddle Peak, which has an elevation of 2,800 feet. More than 55 inches fell in 1978, less than 7 inches in 1961. The data span the seven drought years of 1984 to 1990.

At lower elevations, average temperatures are relatively constant from month-to-month. The ocean creates a layer of moist air over the coast, which diffuses sunlight and further moderates land temperatures. Figure 12 shows average temperatures along the immediate coast and in the mountain interior. Along the ocean, the lowest temperatures average about 10 degrees F warmer in winter, and the highest, about 10 degrees F cooler in summer, than corresponding inland temperatures. At any season, temperatures at most spots in the Santa Monica

Mountains are usually above freezing, so the growing season coincides with the rainy months, from autumn through spring. At the bottom of inland valleys and canyons, however, winter frost is common and sensitive plants, like laurel sumac, can't grow there.

People living within a mile of the beach can enjoy the outdoors most of the year, except during winter storms. In addition, on-shore air flow almost always pushes smog away from the immediate coast. Thus, it is not surprising that many people want to live near or at the beaches, and the land there has become among the most desirable and most expensive in the world.

Because temperatures and pressures are relatively constant, only moderate breezes blow in the mountains for most of the year. In late summer, however, and especially in early fall, Santa Ana winds may sweep away haze and smog. The sky turns a sparkling cobalt above the mountains, dark under their cover of evergreen chaparral, and the blue-green sea fills with whitecaps. In the dry air, my hair flies about and my nose bleeds a bit; those winds make me edgy and anxious, as they do many others.

Storms coming across the Western states pile air

Average Temperatures in the Santa Monica Mountains		
SEASON	IMMEDIATE COAST	MOUNTAIN INTERIOR
Winter	45°F–65°F	35°F–65°F
Summer	60°F–80°F	60°F–90°F

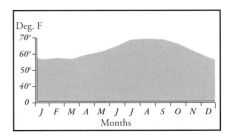

Figure 12: Average temperature by month at low elevations.

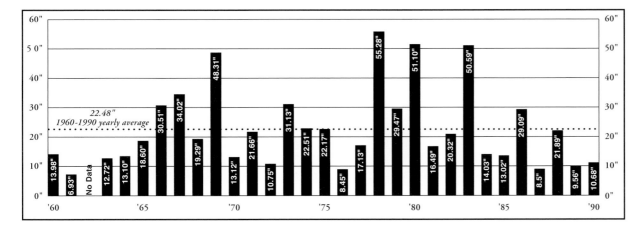

Figure 11: Topanga rainfall 1960-1990.

Helicopter picking up sea water.

RIGHT: Chaparral burning along Pacific Coast Highway, Old Topanga Fire. (JM)

into high-pressure masses, trapped between the Sierra Nevada range and the Rockies. When additional, high-pressure cells block farther, eastward movement, the air flows to the southwest. As it climbs the Sierras, it loses moisture; as it descends to the Mojave Desert, it compresses and heats.

This process repeats when the air passes over and through the Transverse Ranges, and, by the time it reaches the San Fernando Valley it has become the hot, dry Santa Ana wind.

Sometimes during Santa Anas, fires rage across the mountains and burn tens of thousands of acres. In October and November of 1993, clouds of smoke blanketed the mountains and blew over the surrounding ocean and land, dropping ash on hundreds of square miles. For days, helicopters ferried water from reservoirs and the ocean to drop on hot spots. The television crackled with scenes of fleeing people and, at night, walls of flame silhouetted hillside houses before consuming them. Hundreds of millions of dollars worth of property burned.

Typically, fires start during a Santa Ana wind in late October, along roads leading into the mountains. Before the Spanish arrived, California Indians regularly set fires in the flatlands, both in the San Fernando Valley and along the coast in the Los Angeles Basin, which the Spanish called "the Valley of Smokes." But California Indians did not use the Santa Anas to create the devastating wildfires of the twentieth century.

Fires hasten erosion by destroying vegetation that normally holds the soil and by blasting rocks apart. At the same time, recurrent fires have favored those native plants and animals that could evolve strategies to live through it and take advantage of the special conditions it creates.

In spring and early summer, fog often blankets the mountains. When hot, dry air, descending from the Pacific High, meets the ocean, it may create a 2,000-foot thickness of cool, moist air, termed "the

Rock blasted by fire, Mishe Mokwa Trail.

Western fence lizard on lichen-covered rock along Mishe Mokwa Trail.

Fog in Los Liones Canyon.

California sycamores in Sepulveda Pass.

Malibu Canyon.

marine layer," over the immediate coast. The warmer air holds the cool, marine layer beneath, and mountains to the east keep it from moving eastward. Fog forms in the trapped air; within a mile of the coast, this air carries salt.

Day after day, the weather forecast is: "Late night and early morning low clouds and fog along the coast." The monotony of weeks on end of fog and overcast makes me feel as though I live in a blank world without weather, and certainly Los Angeles weather is less extreme than the rest of the U.S., where temperatures can drop 50 degrees in half an hour.

During May and June, and often into July, when the ocean continues to be cool and the land gathers heat, strong sea breezes pile the marine layer to a thickness of 3,000 to 5,000 feet, and low clouds and fog can shroud the land for up to a week at a time. I have become accustomed to missing the fireworks displays along the coast on the Fourth of July. From the Malibu Pier to the Bel Air Bay Club, rockets whoosh up into the fog where their glories burst unseen.

Even so, the fogs have their own charm as they creep up the canyons and sit with our mountains floating above them. Distant ridges become two-dimensional, a series of cutouts against the horizon.

Unfortunately, fog turns to smog over much of the Los Angeles Basin and the San Fernando Valley. Smog makes people sick and can, over the course of years, contribute to their early death. Children in Los Angeles have 20 percent less lung capacity, on average, than do those who live elsewhere in the U.S.

The mountains rise above most of the smog and mountain vegetation helps clean the air. But even a little smog kills lichens, which have no way to filter the air they use. Lichens still thrive far from major roads in Point Mugu State Park.

Most of the streams in the mountains collect run-off during the rainy season from November through April and largely dry up during July through October. Mark Bueller, however, who has hiked the mountains for thirty years, reports that four streams flow all the time, regardless of rainfall: the lowest section of Malibu Creek, Cold Creek, lower Solstice Creek, and the spring in Fryman Canyon, which tumbles down the north slope for the better part of a mile before it disappears underground.

All other streams dry up in late summer and fall during some years, though pools may remain in many. Most flow long enough for animals needing fresh water to complete their life cycles, and enough water remains underground to support streamside trees.

In 1769, Padre Crespi wrote of California sycamores, coast live oaks, white oaks (now called valley oaks), and California walnuts, growing in what must have been our present Sepulveda Pass. All of these trees but the valley oak grow in the pass today, testifying that water is there most of the time, although the only visible stream is at the top, where Mission Canyon drains into the pass.

One stream is unique among those in the mountains—Malibu Creek. For 14 miles, it flows south from the Simi Hills (where it is called Las Virgenes Creek) and cuts entirely through the range to the ocean. Lake Sherwood, Triunfo Creek, and several others drain into Malibu Creek. The drainage has existed since before the current uplift of the range began, five million years ago.

The creek through Cheeseboro Canyon flows under the Ventura Freeway, to the Malibu drainage system. (Confusingly, the California Department of Transportation spells *Cheeseboro, Chesebro.*) For sound ecological reasons, the National Park Service includes this canyon, and adjacent Palo Comado Canyon, in the Santa Monica Mountains National Recreation Area. Natural drainage patterns connect these canyons and Las Virgenes Canyon to the main body of the Santa Monica Mountains.

This drainage bridges islands of open habitat across which plants and animals may move between the Simi Hills and the Santa Monicas, ensuring a more robust diversity of species. There are plans to maintain and improve the exchange of wildlife among these areas by establishing pathways under and over the freeway.

East of Las Virgenes Creek, water drains both north and south from the crest of the range. To the north, storm water runs into the Los Angeles River and then to the ocean. To the south, and as far east as Mandeville Canyon, storm water runs directly from the crest to the sea, supplying sand for beaches rimming Santa Monica Bay.

East of Mandeville, reservoirs and catchment basins collect run-off and release water into storm drains emptying into the bay. Unfortunately, careless misuse of urban gutters and other waterways sometimes pollutes the bay so much it has to be closed to swimmers.

Massive displacements of the earth's crust, scour-

ing winter storms, and raging wildfires are creating the Santa Monica Mountains. The plants, animals, and people in and around the mountains must continue to be able to live and even thrive amid all this violence.

Cold Creek Falls.

Figure 13: Distribution of chaparral in the Santa Monica Mountains. (SWHS)

CHAPTER 3

Chaparral
—Productive Survivor

A ROBE OF CHAPARRAL SPREADS OVER ALMOST ALL OF THE SANTA MONICA MOUNTAINS (as shown on Figure 13). The figure is somewhat misleading, as patches of sage-scrub and oak woodland occur at many places throughout the chaparral.

When the Spanish first approached it, they remembered the thickets of evergreen scrub oaks of Spain and exclaimed, "Ah! *El chaparro!*" Later, gauchos wore leather pants they called *chaparajos*, or "chaps," to thread their way through the dense, prickly bushes.

Only vegetation as hardy as the chaparral could have survived hundreds of thousands of years of recurrent drought, flood, and fire, could have gripped steep slopes whose poverty-stricken soil would otherwise slip away beneath it, and could have lived, all the while, through the attacks of insects and other plant-eaters. Truly, the persistence of the chaparral celebrates the staying power of life.

A nearly impenetrable mass of shrubs identifies the chaparral. These have specialized leaves that pro-duce food year-round because they are evergreen; they are hard, thick and stiff, which makes them strong, conserves moisture and discourages plant-eaters. On drier sites the leaves are usually small, which also saves moisture and reduces absorption of heat during the summer. A number of chaparral shrubs have spiny, tannic, or resinous leaves, further to defend against being eaten.

In the Santa Monica Mountains, the onset of the rainy season marks the beginning of the natural year, for this is when chaparral starts growing. In the year whose tales I tell, rain starts in late November. All through the night it has poured down, deluges interspersed with lighter showers, and in Topanga State Park, the creek in Quarry Canyon is already rushing to empty into Santa Ynez Reservoir.

Only part of the rain is soaking into coarse-textured soil on the ridges above the canyon. The soil contains decomposed, waxy, water-repellent chemicals produced by many chaparral plants, and water runs off the surface until it reaches cracks and crannies.

Growing above the creek are wild lilacs that

Chaparral along Carlisle Canyon.

Rindge wrote of, and they do look like lilacs. They are not true lilacs, however, so gardeners and nurserymen call them by their family name, ceanothus, which I'll use from this point on.

Like many chaparral shrubs, ceanothus has wide-spreading lateral roots to catch surface water seeping into fissures and trickling around the base of trunks. The ability of chaparral shrubs, like ceanothus, to draw up surface water is one feature that makes chaparral so effective in protecting the Santa Monica Mountains watershed.

The pre-dawn is chill under a gray sky, a cold drizzle is falling, and low clouds obscure Temescal Peak. But despite the wet, on a patch of open ground among the ceanothus, a coyote appears to have taken leave of her senses. Repeatedly, she lowers herself to the ground, muzzle upturned, and then, suddenly, lunges sideways and upward several feet. At the top of each leap, her jaws shut with an audible snap. Now and then she stops her odd performance to dig frenziedly, sending up great sprays of uprooted plants and muddy gravel.

She is going after rain beetles, one of her favorite winter meals. Female rain beetles open their burrows to mate during or shortly after the first winter rains. The males fly low over the ground searching for the flightless females, which, still snuggled in their burrows, are wafting rain-beetle perfume. The scent is so alluring that often many males land on a single female and, in their ardor, may tunnel completely through their rivals and even through the female.

If she survives mating, she plugs her burrow with pulverized soil and digs deeper. Her mouth parts, like her mate's, are atrophied, and she cannot eat, but she can live as long as six months on her stored fat. When she has laid her eggs, she dies.

The eggs will hatch the following spring or early summer and the larvae may take as long as ten years to change to adults and mate. Dr. Arthur Evans, Curator of the Insect Zoo at the L.A. Museum of Natural History, reports that the larvae feed only on the roots of ceanothus.

At one point during the coyote's meal, she must stop to defecate, because the outer shells of the beetles affect her gut the way a large dose of bran would. Frank Hovore, an entomologist formerly with the museum, has seen the shells drop in a heap—wings, legs, and all—steaming in the cold air, falling apart like the petals of a black flower, no longer held together inside their devourer.

Coyotes are highly adaptable and inventive and will even play dead to lure vultures close enough to be caught and eaten. Old Man Coyote was one of the main players in the mythology of American Indians, who also called Coyote "The Trickster." Most people know that the coyote is a relative of the wolf and domestic dog.

I pick up my story on a bright, sunny December morning in Cold Creek Preserve, where a side-blotched lizard is basking in an opening in chaparral. During the night, cold air collected in the canyon below the ridge he is on, but he is warming up. Like all reptiles, the temperature of his environment largely determines his body temperature.

Before he can move about to hunt, he must raise his body temperature to a point similar to our own, but he is small enough to heat quickly and can take advantage of short periods of winter warmth like this one. Perhaps this is why the side-blotched lizard is the only kind of lizard in the Santa Monica Mountains that does not hibernate.

Warmed through, he begins looking for the

Coyote. (MP)

Brown rain beetle. (CH)

Side-blotched lizard on Sandstone Peak trail.

Anna's hummingbird. (LS).

Cedar waxwing. (MP)

Toyon in fruit in Marquez Canyon.

43

Deer tick.

insects and other invertebrates that are his prey, darting along the bare ground under chamise and scrub oak, and pausing in sunlit patches to warm again.

In a few minutes he comes upon a deer tick in the dead leaves under a scrub oak, a tick that can carry Lyme disease. It makes a tasty meal for him because it is gorged with the blood of a mule deer.

During December at Charmlee Park, chaparral currant bushes burst with rose-pink blossoms, even though the weather is much too cold for most pollinating insects to be flying. (Like reptiles, invertebrates are cold-blooded.) An Anna's hummingbird flashes over the blooms, laps up the nectar with his long tongue and returns to a perch to utter his squeaky call. It is the only species of hummingbird that calls while perched.

After the autumn, when few plants have been in bloom and most insects have been under cover, this is a welcome feast for the Anna's. And at a time of year when insects are uncommon, the currant might go unpollinated without the Anna's services.

Of the more than 300 species of hummingbird, Anna's is the only one that does not commonly go to Central or South America for the winter. The birds hang around to enjoy the nectar of winter bloomers like the currant, a native plant, and eucalyptus, bottlebrush, tree tobacco, and cape honeysuckle, all of which Europeans brought into southern California. These plants allow the hummers to start nesting as early as December, thereby beating the spring rush. We don't know whether, before people set out plants that bloom in the winter, Anna's hummingbirds went south, as other hummingbirds do.

Insects make up a larger part of their diet than they do for other hummingbirds, and Anna's eat the few insects available when nectar is scarce. To conserve energy, their metabolism slows on cold winter nights.

Early one January morning cedar waxwings are calling with high, thin whistles while they busily strip the plump, red berries from a toyon growing along Topanga Canyon Boulevard. American robins, also winter visitors from farther north, join the waxwings in stuffing themselves on the berries. Coyotes and scrub jays relish the fruit, too, and often divest a heavily laden shrub in a day.

Some people call scrub jays "bluebirds," but bluebirds are quiet and peaceable, unlike these noisy characters. Others call scrub jays "blue jays," a name that belongs to the crested Eastern species.

A few weeks ago, the birds and coyotes ignored the toyon berries, and for good reason—their pulp was poisonous. Now the seeds are ready for planting, the shrub has shifted the poison from pulp to seed and birds find the berries delicious. The poison protects the seeds from being digested; instead, they pass out, unharmed, along with the scat (feces), which adds nutrients to the soil they land in. The late ripening of the berries takes advantage of wintering birds at a time when rains create moist sites for seeds to sprout.

In February, for several weeks, taupish white has dusted the deep olive green of the chaparral above Temescal Canyon, in some places frosting half an acre. Closer, I can make out bouquets of the lacy, white flowers of big-pod ceanothus among the bushes. When the berries fall or are eaten, they leave cups resembling the Mercedes logo, as do berry cups of other kinds of ceanothus.

Spring begins in March, with the onset of warm weather. Within the next three or four months plants will bloom and set seeds, mammals will bear and raise their young, birds will nest, reptiles will mate, and insect larvae will hatch, change to adult form, and start new generations.

Along the Musch Trail at Trippet Ranch, a bower of powder-blue blossoms of greenbark ceanothus sheds a faint scent above the path. Only when the flowers are massed like this can I detect their sweet, buttery odor. But a yellow-faced bumblebee queen needs no such concentration to draw her to gathering pollen and nectar. She is nearly an inch long and is the bumblebee I recognize most easily, with her bright yellow face and thorax and the narrow yellow band around her rear end.

The bumblebee queen is one of the first insects to emerge in the spring because she can warm herself by shivering. All night and on cool days, she has shivered steadily, keeping her thorax and abdomen above 88 degrees F. This allows her to fly at colder temperatures than honeybees, use early-spring and higher-elevation plants more efficiently, and fly early and late in the day and in cloudy weather.

She must work like mad. Before she began to hibernate, drones fertilized her and she is ripe for starting a new colony. She has found a house of a dusky-footed woodrat for her new nest, and is constructing waxen honeypots, filling them with pollen and nectar, building brood cells and laying eggs.

When it is too cold to fly she drapes her plump body over the brood cells and lies facing a honeypot, so closely that she can reach a sugary snack by extending her mouthparts. Her shivering keeps her eggs and young between 75 degrees F and 95 degrees F, even when the surrounding air and the food in her honeypots are only a little above freezing.

Her first offspring will be female workers, much smaller than she. As in a honeybee hive, three kinds of bumblebees will live in the colony: the queen, male drones, and infertile female workers, each with a particular job to do. The queen will continue to construct the egg cells and lay eggs in them and, when necessary, protect the eggs from being eaten by the workers.

The workers will gather nectar and pollen, feed the young, make honeypots, extend and expand old cocoons and brood cells, arrange nesting material, fan the nest when it gets too warm, help incubate the brood, pack pollen in containers, help young adults emerge from their cocoons and clean and prepare old cocoons for food storage. It is not surprising that workers wear themselves out in less than one or two months.

The males have only one assignment—to fertilize the queen.

The yellow-faced bumblebee is one of more than a thousand species of bees native to California. Only a few of them, including bumblebees, are, in the biological sense, social.

Before Europeans brought honeybees to California in 1853, native bees pollinated all of the flowers. Now honeybees pollinate many, especially those grown by farmers.

Bumblebees look more fearsome than honeybees and can sting ferociously and repeatedly, especially in defense of their nest. At other times they are less easily provoked than honeybees, which will sting to drive any potential competitor (including people) away from the flowers they are gathering nectar from. The honeybee sacrifices her life in so doing because her stinger is barbed and rips out of her body to remain in the wound.

The relative tolerance of bumblebees and other native bees for intruders around their food sources lets honeybees keep other bees (and birds) away from food. The result is that honeybees have nearly elimi-

Big-pod ceanothus in bloom, Los Liones trail.

Yellow-faced bumblebee on California buckwheat.

Ceanothus silk moth on ceanothus.

Coyote scat with pits of holly-leaf cherry.

Coyote scat with rodent fur.

nated native bees from some habitats and reduced the variety of pollinators.

To return to my tales. One sunny April day, Louise Sakamoto, a nature-loving friend, and I are hiking on the Backbone Trail. We bend to look at coyote scat and see it's full of holly-leaf cherry pits.

Eating carrion makes coyote scat shiny and dark, and means food is scarce. Eating rodents makes it gray and furry, and means food is plentiful. Like many social mammals, coyotes communicate with odors of urine and scat, which tell their identity and sex and mark their territory. They like to use trails to carry messages.

"In a California Indian myth," I say to Louise, "Old Man Coyote's scat scolds him when he's done wrong and teaches him how to do right."

She laughs. "Mine tells me when I've eaten something I shouldn't have."

Louise hears a tiny rustle beside the trail, leans to search under a sugar bush and lurches back, bumping into me.

"Rattlesnake!" she whispers.

A pattern of dark, light-edged blotches is partly covered by leaves in a sunlit patch about 2 feet off the trail.

"It's not *one* rattlesnake; it's two," I whisper back. "They must be mating."

I squat, to get nearer for a photograph of the snakes, but they sense me and start to slither away.

But not separately. The snake on top drags along the one underneath, thrashing and squirming, until they both disappear down the bank.

"Weird," Louise says. "Why didn't they just uncouple?"

We continue our walk, unaware that the snakes could *not* separate. A forest of stiff, backwardly directed barbs had hooked the male's penis into the female's cloaca. (The cloaca is the duct through which birds, reptiles, and amphibians pass eggs, sperm, and body wastes.)

A couple of hours before we arrived, the enticement from the female's musk glands had drawn the male. Before she would let him insert his menacing, barbed penis, they had engaged in long foreplay, stimulating each other by rubbing under each other's chins and around each other's cloacas.

When they were ready, she rolled on her side, and he lay along her in the dappled sunshine. Then his penis—correction, his two penises—erected. (Actually, each of his two penises forms two branches so that he has four outlets for semen.) He probed her cloaca with the nearest penis and entered. The spines at the base anchored inside her and they had been lying there for over an hour, thrusting and undulating, when we interrupted them.

When we leave, they continue mating. After he inseminates her, his penis will invert, like a finger on a rubber glove, and the spines will fold back so the snakes can separate.

The rattlesnake is the only dangerous reptile in the Santa Monica Mountains. I often see them during April, May, and June, when they are mating and before hot weather sets in.

To avoid jumping toward (or on) a snake, a hiker who hears a rattling sound should stand still until he or she identifies the source. Rattlesnakes prefer to avoid creatures larger than themselves and strike only if stepped on or if they feel severely threatened for some other reason.

For the hiker's own safety, he or she must know the rattler's field marks. The most reliable one is the presence of true rattles, not the rattling sound. The beneficial and harmless gopher snake sometimes makes a sound with its tail that can be mistaken for a rattlesnake.

One morning a few days later, I find three striking moths clinging to the wall outside the door of the Nature Center at Charmlee Park. Colored reddish brown, with creamy white markings, they are male ceanothus silk moths, California's most spectacular moth. The wings of the largest span 5 inches.

Between midnight and dawn, female moths must have been flying about, giving off their perfume to call the males. When they were through mating, the Nature Center light drew the males to settle on the wall next to it.

They will die in a few hours or days, because their mouth parts are atrophied, like those of many moths, and they cannot eat. One can extend their hours of glory by keeping them in a refrigerator and bringing them out briefly for display or picture-taking.

One early May morning, my husband, Jim, Jan Wilson, a hiking friend who teaches nursing, and I are enjoying the spring life along the loop trail above Arroyo Sequit Canyon. The slopes are almost completely covered with chamise in full bloom, bunches of lacy, white flowers set off here and there by fuzzy sprays of wooly blue curls.

In the coolness, birds are flying and calling, looking for food. An Anna's hummingbird squeaks as it chases a black-chinned hummingbird away from the blooms of Indian paintbrush. The black-chin has no intention of lingering, because it's on its way to nest in streamside woodlands, but the belligerent Anna's drives it off anyway. The Anna's bullies all birds, including its own mate and much larger birds, like northern orioles.

Over the millennia, hummingbirds and the plants they pollinate have affected each others' evolution. These birds have no sense of smell, so hummingbird flowers draw them with color, especially red, to which they are most sensitive.

Bees cannot perceive true red but are most sensitive to ultraviolet, which we cannot see. Thus, the red of hummingbird flowers separates the birds from the bees and helps ensure that the pollen reaches its intended goal, another flower of the same kind. Hummingbird flowers put their pollen where it will stick to the bird and secrete their nectar where only hummingbirds' long tongues can reach it.

However, many red flowers attract both hummingbirds and bees. Such flowers always have a tinge of blue or invisible ultraviolet.

Flower mites live on, and in, paintbrush nectar. These relatives of spiders are the size of a printed period. When the paintbrush blossom fades, the mites, too little to go very far on their own, must move to a new source of nectar or die.

Enter the Anna's hummingbird. Each time it thrusts its bill into the paintbrush blossom, some of the flower mites run up the bill and settle in the bird's nostrils. When the bird visits another bloom, the mites race down the bill and land in a fresh source of nectar. In this way the bird services both the flower and its mites.

A feast of song accompanies Jan, Jim, and me on our walk: California thrashers, house finches, and wrentits, all busily defending their territories. Wrentits are very shy and usually hide inside their favorite bush, no matter how hard we try to see them.

At this time of year, though, they are aggressive and will even sing from an exposed perch. To see if he can draw the wrentit out, Jim makes squeaking noises with his lips. Sure enough, a little, long-tailed, dark

Rattlesnake, Charmlee Park.

Wrentit. (MP)

Chamise and wooly bluecurls in bloom in Arroyo Sequit.

Indian paintbrush blooming along trail to Nicholas Flat.

California quail. (MP)

bird appears out of the chamise and makes passes at his head.

The wrentit is not a tit, for more reasons than the obvious one. Tits are a family of mainly Old World birds to which chickadees belong. In this usage, "tit" is a respectable word, coming from the Old Icelandic *titr*, meaning "something small," which the wrentit surely is.

Not only is the wrentit not a tit, it is not a wren, either. Its common name is a good example of the way early European explorers applied the names of birds they knew to the unfamiliar birds of North America.

Wrentits live only in the chaparral along the west coast of California and Baja California. They are most easily identified by their song (sometimes called "the voice of the chaparral"), on the same pitch, a series of loud, ringing whistles that run together at the end, with a rhythm similar to that of a bouncing ping-pong ball.

"Did you know the female sings only the first part of the song?" Jan says.

I didn't, but farther along the trail we hear just a few whistles on one side of the path. Jan smiles when, what must be a male, replies with the second part from the *other* side.

"A wrentit duet!" I say.

Then Jim tells us about the wrentits in the early years of sound films, when many movies were made in the chaparral near Los Angeles. Producers did not realize that the wrentit's voice anchored the scenes firmly on the west coast of California, so wrentit voices accompanied stories that were supposed to take place on the East Coast or in Egypt or India.

"For a few years, the wrentit was the most widely distributed bird in the world!" Jim finishes.

We see a pair of California quail walking silently over the leaf litter beneath the shrubs, perhaps looking for a nest site. The winter rains have been unusually abundant and the quail are sleek and perky from their diet of lush herbs growing along the trail. This spring they will raise a large brood, whereas during the drought years they had few or no chicks. Biologists have found that stunted plants growing during drought accumulate hormones that act as a natural birth control for California quail.

Now, reluctant to fly as always, they continue to walk away soundlessly, jaunty black plumes tilted forward from the tops of their heads. We approach close enough to see the black throat and face and white necklace of the handsome male without using our binoculars, and still they do not fly.

As they walk out of sight among the trunks and ribbons of the red shank, from across the canyon rings the distinctive call of another male: *ki-CAH-ko*. It's easy for me to remember the quail's call because it sounds like "Chi-CA-go" in English or *"cui-DA-do"* ("careful!") in Spanish.

My next story takes place one summer night in the Goat Buttes above Malibu Creek. A dainty little California mouse about to give birth to her second litter of the year, curls into her nest near the outside of a dusky-footed woodrat's house.

In the cold air that has crept up Malibu Canyon from the distant ocean, her mate snuggles against her, nose twitching, big, liquid eyes watching her clean each baby as it appears and even giving a lick to the little ones that are already suckling. In a few minutes, four tiny bodies press against her soft, white belly, little tails twirling.

The California mouse lives only in mature chaparral and depends on dense brush for food and protection. It is one of several species of mouse native to the Santa Monica Mountains and often lives in woodrat nests.

Throughout the night, mother mouse moves about their apartment with babies hanging tightly on her nipples. After giving birth, changes in her hormonal balance as well as the babies' suckling stimulate the flow of milk and alter her behavior.

Milk feeds the baby mice and protects them from disease. Also, milk and their sucking raise their body temperature until they can control it themselves. And because the mother's nipples are on her belly, her body protects her brood both from exposure to cold

and rain and from predators.

As well as providing comfort, heat, and food to her offspring, she will be hostile toward other adult mice except her mate. The altered hormonal balance and the production of another hormone, which is stimulated by suckling, cause this hostility and are partly responsible for what we call "the maternal instinct."

Mother mouse keeps up her strength by nibbling the flowers and seeds she and her mate have stashed in the nest. She and father mouse have formed a bond that will last as long as they both survive.

About an hour after the babies are born father mouse creeps outside to forage, leaving his family behind. Just before dawn, he returns with extra food stuffed in his cheeks.

The woodrat landlady ventures out to eat leaves, seeds, and berries. For several hours she feeds, creeping through the chaparral, climbing bushes with new foliage and exploring fissures in the volcanic buttes in which she has wedged her messy home.

For most city dwellers, *rat* evokes a shuddery vision of the Norway rat, a disease-bearing creature of filth that one mammal specialist called "the most unpleasant mammal in the world." The dusky-footed woodrat is, in fact, about the same size as the Norway rat but is a quite different animal. For one thing, it is attractive, with soft fur and large, black eyes. It prefers to live in its own home, which it builds from sticks and other materials, it does not infest crops or stored foods, nor is it a reservoir of age-old human diseases, like typhus and plague.

Many other species besides California mice and bumblebees may live in the woodrat's house, which may be 6 feet high. To construct the nest, the woodrat uses whatever it can carry—sticks, rocks, cacti, cow

Dusky-footed woodrat nest near Dead Horse trail.

Dusky-footed woodrat. (MP)

Red shank, Mishe Mokwa trail.

patties, tin cans.

Some people call the woodrat a "pack rat" because it will take an object, such as a camp knife, and leave a stick or something else in its place. It is not paying for what it took, however. Instead, because it cannot carry more than one object at a time it simply drops the less desirable one and carries off the one it prefers.

Around 8 a.m., the California mice hear the woodrat return and silence falls over the dwelling. Then, near noon, the mice hear a rustling and smell a strange odor from the passage next to them. Unlike a woodrat rustle, the sound seems to glide or, yes, to slither; the scent is a snake's.

Mother mouse will have to get out to save herself and her offspring. Babies clinging to her nipples, she creeps along another runway in the woodrat pile, peers outside and checks that the hole she remembered under a nearby ceanothus bush is within dashing distance. She makes a run for it, babies bumping and rustling underneath, and pops into the hole.

Fortunately, no snakes live in it—only some beetles and spiders. Unfortunately, one of the babies has fallen off during her headlong flight.

When the snake, a California striped racer, emerges from the escape route he spots the squirming baby mouse and gulps it down. Then he burrows under leaf litter to digest his meal.

One late afternoon in September, I spot yellow-rumped warblers scouring a scrub oak at Trippet Ranch for insects. (Mary Valentine calls them "butter butts." She's an archaeologist and naturalist friend.) These birds nest in the high mountains, and large flocks spend the winter along the coast and in the Santa Monicas.

Neither the birds nor I notice several leafwing moths on the oak because the moths remain motionless, relying on their resemblance to dead leaves to escape detection. When daylight has gone, the moths take off to look for California redberry and other shrubs to lay their eggs on.

One of the moths has been flying about for more than an hour when she hears the faint, high chittering of a canyon bat in front of her. Immediately she reverses course and speeds away in the other direction.

About 300 yards from her, her sister hears the same chittering, but to her it is very loud because the bat is nearby. She dips, soars and turns as fast as she can, and the chittering fades. Her tactic has also been successful.

Unlike most insects, some moths have earlike structures that are tuned to bat frequencies. When they hear a bat, they try to escape in one of two ways, depending on how close the bat is. If it is far enough away, they can fly away from it, but if it is close it can easily overtake them. Therefore, when a loud sound indicates a bat is near, they dodge and zigzag so it won't have a straight run at them.

As a submarine uses sonar to find a target, bats find their prey by sending out sounds that objects reflect back to the bat. The reflected sound tells the bat how far away the object is, which way it is moving with respect to the bat, and how fast.

The canyon bat is the smallest bat in the United

Gray foxes. (NPS)

States. Dr. Linda Barkley, a mammal specialist, was working with some of the several species of bats living in the mountains before she left the L.A. County Museum of Natural History. Of those she told me about, the canyon bat is the one I've seen most often because it flies in early evening.

On a cold, blustery night, in late December, a gray fox settles below the Goat Buttes to eat a dusky-footed woodrat. The wind ruffles his fur and hurls a few drops of rain on the remains of the woodrat's house, which the fox has scattered about. Several hundred feet away in a cave in the Goat Buttes a coyote's snout twitches. Perhaps somewhere in her memory rain beetles are flying.

With the arrival of rain, plants and animals of the chaparral begin another year, a year that may be as usual as the one just past or that may bring floods, fires, or earthquakes to the mountain dwellers.

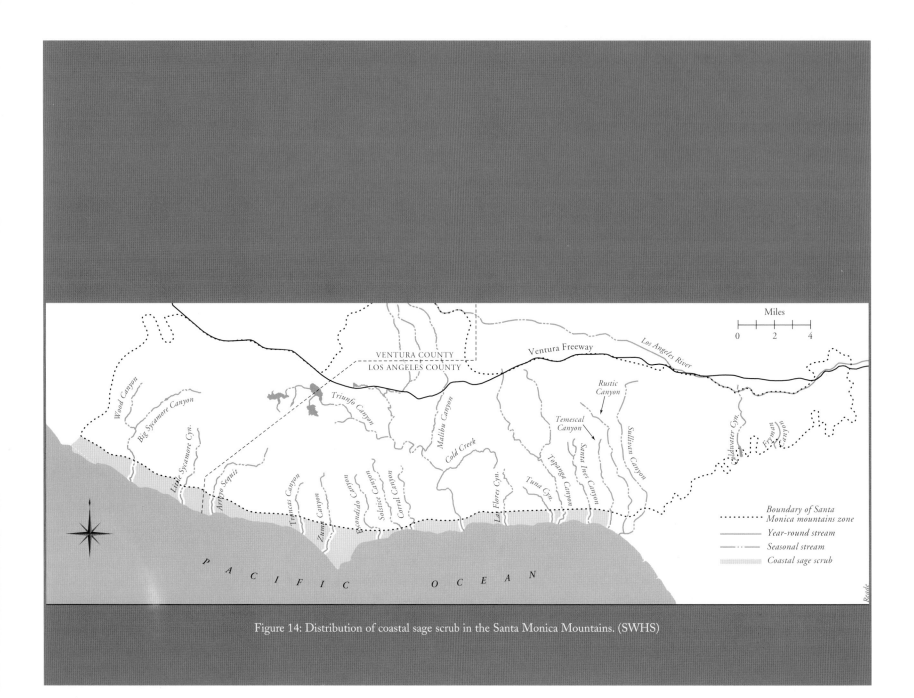

Figure 14: Distribution of coastal sage scrub in the Santa Monica Mountains. (SWHS)

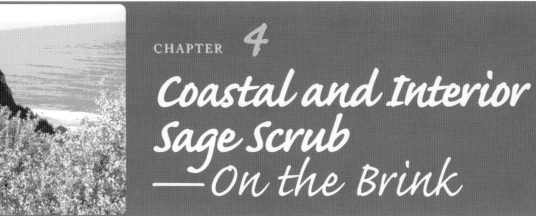

CHAPTER *4*

Coastal and Interior Sage Scrub
—On the Brink

COASTAL AND INTERIOR SAGE SCRUB HANGS *ON IN THE MOST STRESSFUL ENVIRONMENT* in the Santa Monica Mountains: steep slopes or rocky cliffs at low elevations where average rainfall is scant. Though south-facing areas next to the ocean are often fogged in, they are considerably drier than those higher up, which get nearly twice as much rainfall. Even less rain falls on low-elevation slopes inland because the mountains have squeezed most of the water out of the passing air.

In addition, because the Santa Monica Mountains are still rising, there are few places where erosion has had time to deposit deep soils that could hold rain water. Therefore, except beneath streambeds, ground water will have run off and, by mid-June, most lower slopes will be almost completely dry.

Today most sage scrub borders the immediate coast, though sixty years ago, large patches also occurred inland, and shreds of the inland ecosystem remain. Because the coastal and interior ecosystems differ in several details, I'll refer to both together as "sage-scrub" from this point on.

Here, plants and resident animals have only a few months to grow and reproduce—late winter through late spring; by June, the sun is so hot that most life is in danger of cooking. At the peak of the growing season, however, sage-scrub can put on beautiful displays.

Sage-scrub bushes are shorter (1 to 7 feet tall) than chaparral shrubs and not as dense or rigid, often with bare ground between them. Many are leafless during the summer drought. California sagebrush, an aromatic member of the sunflower family that is not a true sage, usually dominates the ecosystem, hence the name.

When I walk among sage-scrub plants (which I cannot in chaparral), piquant aromas often float around me, even when I can see no flowers. The scents arise from compounds similar to those found in thyme, kitchen sage, and rosemary. Biologists are not sure what these compounds do for plants. They may protect them from foliage-eaters, retard growth of competing plants, reduce water loss, or all three.

Pygmy blue butterfly near Malibu Lagoon.

Giant coreopsis in bloom near Zuma.

Salt bush along the Pacific Coast Highway.

Many areas that would support sage-scrub are especially attractive for agriculture because they are relatively flat and easy to get to from the San Fernando Valley or L.A. Basin. By sixty years ago, Europeans had converted much of the ecosystem to farming and ranching.

In addition, the views are often spectacular, which encourages urban and suburban home building. As a result, sage-scrub is an endangered ecosystem in the Santa Monica Mountains and plants and animals requiring it to survive are pressured as well.

The competition for habitat between the California gnatcatcher and people who want golf courses has had widespread publicity. Though no sightings of the bird in the Santa Monicas have been verified, other, unpublicized animals and plants are also threatened. Coastal scrub oak, which grows only on bluffs, headlands, and hillsides within sight of the ocean, is in danger and is probably the rarest of the shrub oaks. The California horned lizard, desert woodrat, black-tailed jack rabbit, and coastal western whiptail lizard are also in precarious straits in the

Santa Monicas.

Not only plants and animals, but people can be at risk as well. Those homes with the fantastic views sometimes fall down cliffs during earthquakes or heavy rains or are engulfed by fire roaring up the slope.

Now I'll tell you some stories about what happens to sage-scrub residents as the natural year progresses. Right after the first rains, usually in November or December, plants surge with growth and, by February, within a mile of the ocean, several kinds of saltbush and pigweed are thriving. In these locations, salt precipitates from the ocean air and sinks into the soil, where it steals water from the roots of most plants, making it even harder for them to survive in this dry habitat. But the salty taste of the leaves of pigweed and saltbush shows how they cope with so much salt—they simply sweat it out through special glands in their leaves.

These leaves feed the larvae of the pygmy blue, North America's smallest butterfly with a wing span of about half an inch.

By March, some plants are either blooming or just on the verge of it. After a few warm days I drive along PCH looking for the eye-catching yellow flowers of giant coreopsis that pop out on bluffs and at the mouths of canyons. Its intensely green, feathery foliage sets off the blooms like a floral bouquet.

I sometimes find tiny nests decorated with spiderwebs, feathers, and lichens, the work of female Costa's hummingbirds. I like to imagine that these little birds are proud of their work, but it has a more practical consequence. It helps me tell the nests of Costa's from those of Anna's hummingbirds.

Normally a desert dweller, a few Costa's stay in the sage-scrub all winter, and others may move here from the desert in the summer to raise a second brood. Very rarely, this species hybridizes with Anna's.

In April, before the yucca starts to flower, yucca moths emerge from their pupas in the soil at the base of the plants and mate, setting in motion one of the best-known examples of mutualism. When the yucca blooms, a pregnant female gathers sticky pollen from one blossom, forms it into a ball and carries it to another blossom. After she presses the ball into the cup-shaped stigma, the female part of the flower, she descends to the base of the ovary, cuts a slit in it with little cutters on her egg-laying organ and lays about half a dozen eggs inside.

Before her eggs hatch, the yucca ovary will produce nutritious seeds because she has pollinated it and her caterpillars will have plenty to eat as they grow. She lays only a few eggs per yucca ovary and a large fraction of the seeds will mature normally. It is as though the yucca moth can foresee the results of her actions, though we know her apparent intelligence must be stored in her genes.

When the larvae have shed their skins three times, they bore holes in the ovary wall, climb out and fall to the ground, where they dig in, make chrysalises and pupate. After a year, they emerge to mate.

Without yucca moths, yuccas cannot set seed and can reproduce only by pups, rosettes that form at the base when the yucca dies. Without yuccas, the moths would have no food for their young. The process binds each species of yucca moth to a particular species of yucca.

On a sunny April morning on the slopes above Thornhill Broome Beach, a female greater bee fly hovers in front of black sage blossoms. Looking like a fuzzy, squat bee, she clings on a bloom and inserts her

Burned home in Old Topanga Canyon.

Yucca Moth placing pollen on stigma. (DF)

Sara orange-tip butterfly. (JL)

Deerweed bloom, Arroyo Sequit.

Digger bee colony, Mishe Mokwa trail.

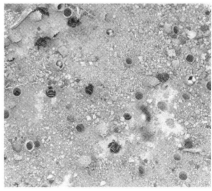

proboscis deep inside, drinks some nectar, then moves to another flower, pollinating it as she feeds.

A female digger bee buzzes up and pushes the smaller bee fly away from the blossom. The digger bee, which looks like a small honeybee, is one of several native, solitary bees that nest in clay or sand. After gathering nectar and pollen, the digger bee flies to a dirt bank above PCH, where she has excavated her nest and laid an egg in it.

I happened to be sitting on the bank, taking pictures of paintbrush, when I noticed several bees and bee flies flying about me and discovered I was in the midst of twenty-two digger bee nests. Biologists are investigating the reasons for such clustering by bees that are not social in the biological sense.

The bee fly follows the digger bee and joins other bee flies, waiting for the digger bees to open their passageways and put honey and pollen in the cells.

California buckwheat, Charmlee Park.

When the digger bee leaves her nest, the bee fly dives down and shoots her own eggs into the entrance. Her larvae will hatch and fatten on the digger bee larvae.

Parasites (actually, parasitoids, in this case) like these are essential to the natural world. They increase the diversity of species by holding in check a few insects that might out-compete most of the others. But nest parasites revolt my mammalian self because they destroy defenseless young and take advantage of the dedicated labors of the parents.

One sunny May morning, I'm out with Mary Valentine, who lives above Arroyo Sequit Canyon and has taught me a lot about spiders and insects. She exclaims with delight when a male, sara orange-tip butterfly flashes by and pauses to sip at the yellow blossoms of deer weed. She tells me the orange-tip has come from the second brood this year. The chrysalides, from the larvae he sires, will overwinter to produce the first brood next year and bring with them a sure sign of spring.

Some of the flowers on the deer weed are yellow, and some, deep orange. When an insect pollinates a flower, the flower turns orange, a color that does not attract insect pollinators as yellow does. This helps ensure that pollinators concentrate their efforts where they will do most good.

Deer weed contributes to life in the sage-scrub from bottom to top. It's in the pea family, and its roots, like those of its relatives, harbor bacteria that fix nitrogen in the soil. It is among the first shrubs to colonize disturbed ground and keep soil from running down the slope.

Its foliage is rich in nitrogen and its nectar and pollen feed a host of insects: bees of all kinds and several kinds of butterflies as well as the sara orange-tip. Deer also like to browse its flowers and leaves.

It grows in a weedy fashion but, in view of its general usefulness and the pretty show it makes in full bloom, Mary and I agree it's a far cry from a noxious weed.

I find a ladybug sitting on the leaves of a black sage that is just coming into bloom. (The British, as well as entomologists, call ladybugs "ladybird beetles." I eschew such an affectation.) This is one of several hundred ladybugs that have been hibernating since December on the cool floor of Trancas Canyon, and have scattered to look for aphids and other insects tender new growth attracts.

Sure enough, the upper surface of a few leaves is very shiny and sticky. I turn the sticky leaves over and find fat, green aphids, the ladybugs' favorite prey, underneath. While we watch, they creep toward whatever shade they can find: the other side of the leaf or even the tiny shadow cast by the leaf rib. They are surely trying to hide from the bright sun, which would quickly cook their soft bodies.

The pungent odor of the black sage leaves reminds me of the sage people use to flavor fish and chicken. Kitchen sage is closely related to black sage, and I use black sage leaves the same way.

On a June morning, along the Santa Ynez fire road, blooms of California buckwheat, one of the most characteristic plants of sage-scrub, make a nearly solid bank of light pink. A continuous drone rises above the puff-shaped blossoms, where honeybees are gathering nectar. Honey connoisseurs rate buckwheat honey as exceptionally fine and buckwheats are the largest source of honey in the U.S.

I search the flowers in vain for little Acmon blue butterflies, which also prefer the nectar of buckwheat and deer weed. The honeybees must have driven them off, but I find a few tiny, sluglike larvae eating

Greater bee fly.

Bush sunflower in bloom in Temescal Canyon.

Same view with dormant bush sunflower.

Dormant giant coreopsis, Pacific Coast Highway.

the blossoms.

A flurry of gravel near my feet startles me as a lizard zips under the buckwheat. I kneel, to see which one it is, and discover a whiptail lizard with orangeish striping down its back and a pretty black-and-white checkered pattern on side of its throat and neck.

There's no way I can tell by the markings whether it's male or female. My friend, Dr. Lee Kats, a tall, gracious scientist who specializes in amphibians and reptiles, points out that some species of whiptail are all female and reproduce asexually but ours isn't one of these.

A sharp sting on my ankle sends me leaping to my feet, and I stamp several times to shake three California harvester ants off my socks. Too intent on the whiptail, I hadn't noticed the ants going in and out of a crater in loose soil beneath the buckwheat. They are carrying buckwheat seeds into the nest and

Roadrunner. (NPS)

a drift of discarded, reddish brown hulls covers the soil nearby.

As I proceed along the bank, I scare up two more whiptails within 20 feet of each other. The fine crop of insects on the buckwheat this morning must have drawn them here. Next month, they will retreat to their burrows during the heat of mid-day and come out only in the morning and evening.

On my way back to my car, I meet a youngster who thrusts something at me. "Look," he says, proffering a dusty hand. "A horney toad."

"Isn't it weird!" I exclaim. "May I hold it?" I reach out my hand.

He withdraws it, disappointment clouding his tanned face. "Aren't you scared of it?"

"Did you know it eats ants?"

"Yeah?" He looks doubtful.

"Yes. There's an ant nest on the bank back there. Let's watch it."

"It'll get away."

I hope. "You can always catch it again."

I start toward the harvester ants, the horned lizard's favorite prey. "Where'd you find it?"

"It was just sitting by the trail."

"They like to sun themselves. They think you won't see them because of their camouflage."

No wonder horned lizards are uncommon. They're easy to catch in the open, sandy areas they like, and, like the whiptail and some snakes and birds, enjoy basking in open areas in the sage-scrub and need the loose, dry soil for burrowing.

He puts the lizard on top of the ants, keeping hold of its tail, but it is motionless.

"You should let it go, you know," I say.

"Naw." He makes a face at me.

"There's no way you can gather enough ants to feed it. Besides, it's against the law to collect it."

"I know," I go on. "Why don't you go to the pet store and buy something weirder." I rummage five dollars out of my fanny pack.

He grins and lets go the tail to take the money and I'm happy to see my horned lizard scamper off.

Horned lizard, camouflaged on ground. (LS)

By late July, sage-scrub is an almost uniform, earth-brown and appears lifeless under the hot sun, because of the tactics plants have evolved for surviving the long, rainless summer. Some, like bush sunflower, simply go dormant and leave their dead foliage hanging on brown stems. Stands of beautiful giant coreopsis now look like groves of brown floor mops sticking up above bare ground.

Others, such as California poppy, die to the ground. Some have a rootstock that will recreate the plant when winter rains come. Succulents like coastal prickly pear, yucca and chalk live-forever store water in thick, fleshy roots and leaves, and laurel sumac leaves toughen to reduce evaporation and make them harder for insects to eat. Not surprisingly, deer and other plant eaters avoid sage-scrub during this time.

In early August, I take my morning hike up the

steep, switchbacked trail in Los Liones Canyon, conditioning myself for an upcoming, extended hiking trip. Just before the trail meets the Santa Ynez fire road, it emerges from dense, ceanothus chaparral into sage-scrub.

This morning, I see a roadrunner just beyond the ceanothus, sitting in the middle of the trail, with its wings and tail spread out, sunning itself. It hasn't seen me, and I watch it for several minutes while it basks and preens.

As I watch, I can't help thinking about the roadrunner's animated cartoon persona—whirling down the road with neck outstretched and going "beep, beep." The artists only partly capture the bird's full comical essence. People have seen it stop suddenly, raise its neck, erect its scruffy crest and cock its head sideways. Then it pumps its tail up, lets it fall slowly, and pumps it again. (No explanation for this odd behavior is given.) It usually flattens its topknot while running; with each stop, it appears to swell as it opens its wings and erects its tail, crest, and body feathers.

Though a competent flier, it seldom flies but runs after prey at speeds up to 15 miles per hour. It earned its common name in the early days from its habit of running down the road ahead of horse-drawn carriages, with its feet barely touching the ground and its wings and tail used for balance and maneuver.

Roadrunners mate for life and both parents incubate the eggs and care for the young. Such dedication and constancy make roadrunners seem more serious than the nutty character of the cartoons.

Biologists aren't sure why roadrunners and many other birds sun themselves. Perhaps the sun's warmth activates lice and mites and makes them easier for the birds to find and pick off. Or could it be that the warmth simply gives the birds pleasure, as it does

people and other animals?

Now, the nights are warm enough for Jim and me to camp under the oaks at Point Mugu State Park. In the late afternoon, we backpack our gear from the Ray Miller trailhead 2 miles into La Jolla Valley campground. As canyon bats snag flying insects over the trail, we heat macaroni and cheese on our Coleman stove. (The Park Service permits no ground fires in this dry country.) After a good meal, we sip coffee and talk ourselves to sleep under a sky full of oak leaves.

I wake after midnight, annoyed by a dream of not being able to find a ladies' room, get out of my sleeping bag and start toward the facility. I paint the path ahead with the beam of my flashlight, though the moonlight is almost bright enough by itself to walk by.

Then I stop, astonished. Pale, little creatures are soundlessly dancing across the trail in front of me, like a troop of tiny ghosts. They are Pacific kangaroo rats, hopping in the moonlight, perhaps drawn by the aroma of our dinner. Slowly I swing my light onto them, and their enormous, liquid eyes shine at me, like orange headlights on miniature jeeps.

I creep back to where Jim is sleeping to share my discovery, and when we return to the trail, the dancers are closer to our camp. Though we know they would like some of our trail mix, we don't feed them. We don't want to encourage them to depend on handouts from campers, or get into trouble with someone who would abuse them.

Kangaroo rats are much more closely related to ground squirrels and pocket gophers than to rats. Like their cousins, they live in deep burrows with several chambers for sleeping, nesting, and storing food, which they carry in fur-lined, external cheek pouches.

Like many inhabitants of the sage-scrub, they

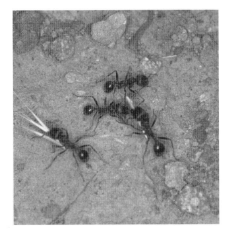

Harvester ants, Mishe Mokwa trail.

Chia bloom.

Tarantula hawk wasp on scale broom, Zuma Canyon.

Ctenucha moth, Santa Ynez fire road.

Tarantula, Santa Ynez fire Road.

can survive in the desert as well. They go into their burrows to escape heat and need little or no water because they produce it from the seeds they consume.

Among these are seeds of laurel sumac, a common bush of the coastal sage scrub.

In the fall, the seed-heads of California buckwheat rim the sage-scrub with warm, reddish brown banks of color, and stalks of purple, black, and white sage bear whorls of seed pods. The copious seeds of chia, another kind of sage, are particularly rich in protein. According to legend, a teaspoonful could sustain a person for twenty-four hours on a forced march. This may have been true, because liquid makes the seeds swell and fill one's stomach. California Indians used chia seeds as a dietary staple, beating them out of the seed-heads into baskets.

Chia is now rare in our mountains, probably because of suburban development and the cessation of deliberate burning of chia-gathering areas by California Indians. Even so, seeds of the sage-scrub are still a bounty for resident small birds—savannah sparrows, house finches, lesser goldfinches, and bushtits—and for migrants—white-crowned sparrows, dark-eyed juncos, and lazuli buntings.

Scale broom, a shrub with scaly leaves and brush-like, yellow flowers, is blooming in the sandy wash along Zuma Canyon. I have come here, one October day, to photograph ctenucha (pronounced "te-noó-ka") moths that Mary Valentine has told me are fond of this plant. These beautiful, day-flying moths resemble wasps that birds and lizards don't like to eat.

A tarantula hawk flashes orange wings as it zooms under one of the bushes, where it has found a tarantula. The body of this enormous wasp is more than 2 inches long.

The tarantula, a male with legs spanning more than 6 inches, faces the wasp and threatens it with his front appendages. (These look like a fifth pair of legs but are not true legs.) The tarantula hawk attacks, and the tarantula grabs her steely-blue body and sinks his fangs in, injecting venom.

Though Art Evans has told me the wasp usually wins a contest like this, I root for the spider, which is harmless to people unless severely provoked. I know too

well that if the tarantula hawk succeeds in paralyzing him, she will lay an egg on him and he will be immobilized while her grub devours him. If that happens, will he face days of agony?

The wasp pulls free and attacks from the rear, where she stings the spider. He writhes around, clutches her and bites her again. She must be missing his nerve centers because the battle continues for a full five minutes, each combatant biting and stinging the other, each moving more and more slowly.

At last, the tarantula hawk is too exhausted and full of venom to move, and the tarantula crawls away to rest.

Tarantulas, horned lizards, kangaroo rats, coastal scrub oaks—these are some of the fascinating animals and plants that still survive in what remains of this very special threatened ecosystem.

Pacific kangaroo rat. (HP)

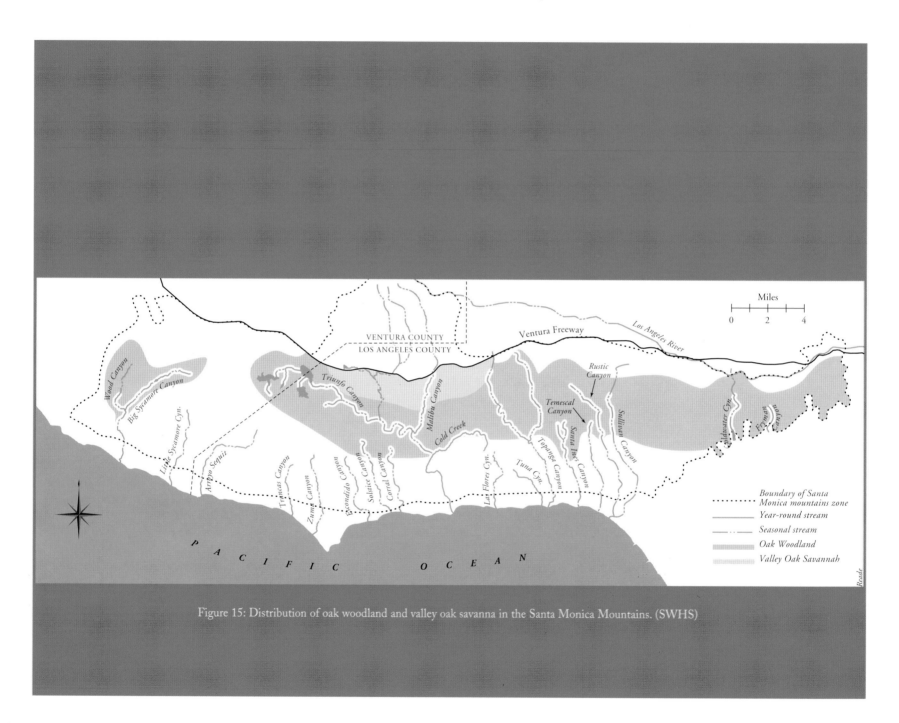

Figure 15: Distribution of oak woodland and valley oak savanna in the Santa Monica Mountains. (SWHS)

CHAPTER 5
Oak Woodland and Valley Oak Savanna
—Old California

WOODLAND? BUT SOUTHERN CALIFORNIA IS TOO DRY FOR WOODLANDS.

Most of the trees in the city have been brought in. Tall conifers cap the high mountains to the east but they're remote from L.A. woodlands—towering, green, lining roads, blanketing hills—are what many newcomers miss in the countryside around L.A.

I yearned for forests when I moved here. Imagine my surprise during my first visit back East to discover that the endless trees suffocated me. I had grown to need the openness of California. That openness helps give southern California culture its "anything-goes" flavor.

Here, grasslands and woodlands go together because each requires deeper soils and more moisture than do chaparral and sage-scrub. In fact, grasslands often infiltrate woodlands or form savannas—open areas dotted by trees. Figure 15 shows the general distribution of woodlands and savannas in the Santa Monica Mountains. Patches of these ecosystems also occur within each other and within chaparral and sage-scrub.

Except near water, woodlands in southern California are oak woodlands. Among the most beautiful sights nature has to offer, groves of majestic, rounded oaks, some nearly 100 feet tall, or with massive limbs spreading more than 200 feet, nestle in moist canyons or spring from deep soil. Thick canopies are alive with birds, the cool shade an escape during the summer drought.

Oaks have long blessed the Santa Monica Mountains. Perhaps five thousand years ago, California Indians discovered that oaks supplied food, in the form of acorns, as well as tools, fuel, and other needs. For millennia, Europeans revered oaks and, in years past, worshiped the noble soul of the tree. In fact, the scientific name for the oak family, *Quercus*, comes from two Celtic words: *quer*, meaning fine and *cuez*, meaning tree.

It's no wonder the first European settlers built their ranch houses among oaks where they turned grasslands into pastures. But, since then, wood cutting and development have destroyed extensive

Coast live oak woodland, Topanga State Park.

stands of trees. Now, with freeways and subdivisions covering the land, the wonder is that any remain. Public agencies have set aside some of these for people like me and my friends to stroll in and enjoy a picnic lunch beneath the huge old trees, bark gray with lichen, and defend our sandwiches from feisty scrub jays.

Coast live oaks comprise almost all of the oak woodlands in the Santa Monicas. The statelier valley oak grows mostly in valley oak savannas on the inland side of the mountains from Encino westward.

Coast live oak is the only oak tree that grows well along the coast, in places where it is out of reach of salt-laden air and wind. It is evergreen (hence, "live oak"), reaches 20 to 40 feet tall, and can have a trunk as much as 6 feet around.

Repeated burning has bent many of these old trees. Thick bark insulates the trunk from all but the hottest fires, and dormant buds in the regenerating layer have used food stored in the roots to grow branchlets and foliage. By now, a twisted superstructure of heavy, gnarled limbs and branches and multiple trunks, some of which may grow horizontally, impart an other-worldly atmosphere to coast live oak

woodlands. A dense, dark green, leafy helmet is home to animals ranging from moth larvae to gray squirrels. The oval leaves are small, thick, hard, and usually convex; I imagine them as tiny boats bobbing along a spring freshet.

When the November sun first glints over the ridge above Encinal Canyon, its pale light reveals shadows of four mule deer, moving in the grove of coast live oaks in Charmlee Park. The doe stretches her neck and lifts her moist muzzle to pull ripe acorns off a lower branch. Her fawn is nosing among leaf litter, searching for nuts that have fallen, and her two yearling offspring are stripping a scrub oak growing on the edge of the grove. As the family eats, breaths steaming in the cool, damp air, the only sound is of the surf, less than 2 miles away.

A sudden rustle above her head startles the fawn into looking into the leaves. She sees a western gray squirrel running along a bough. It sits to nibble a rich, reddish brown nut between its forepaws, thick, brushy tail flashing silky in the morning sun. Like the deer, the squirrel relies on acorns to store fat for the coming winter.

"Wá-ka! Wá-ka!" Several voices rattle the

Western gray squirrel. (MP)

Acorn woodpecker on granary tree. (BS)

Scrub jay. (BS)

Female trapdoor spider. (CH)

Trapdoor spider door. (CH)

canopy, but neither squirrel nor deer are upset. Acorn woodpeckers have been gathering the crop for more than a week, eating the nuts or stockpiling them, for the time when their other fare of berries, insects, and tree sap will be in short supply.

Black wings and rump flashing white, a male flies off with an acorn in his large, strong beak. He heads northwest, into Lachusa Canyon, and searches briefly along the surface of a sycamore. One branch is already studded with acorns, but he discovers an empty hole and pushes the nut in. By the end of the harvest, he will have stored a few hundred acorns in the granary that his family group of ten birds share and protect. Acorn woodpeckers make granaries in poles or trees with soft, thick bark, such as sycamore or valley oak. Mark Bueller says the birds often use branches on more than one tree.

By the time the woodpecker starts back to the grove, patches of sunshine are warming the ground. The squawk of a female scrub jay greets him. She plucks an acorn, lights in poison oak along one side of the grove, hops down, and pounds the nut into the earth.

Unlike the woodpecker, she may forget where she stashed this acorn, or where she buried more than half of the thousands she will stockpile this season. Her poor memory (as well as that of squirrels and other rodents) is vital to oaks. Buried acorns are more likely to escape being eaten and to germinate than those on the surface. And, by moving many acorns away from the parent plant, jays expand the grove and reduce competition with other seedlings.

A covey of quail, uttering soft chucks, is also enjoying the bounty. Quail, deer, and gray squirrels depend so heavily on acorns that a poor crop can cause many to starve to death before spring.

By late November, when cold, rainy weather sets in, almost all the acorns have been eaten or stockpiled. Now the deer stretch for mistletoe and lichens, which they prefer above all other browse. Mistletoe is a true parasite that weakens trees by sucking water and minerals from under the bark. One kind of mistletoe grows only on oaks, whereas another grows on several other kinds of trees.

One rainy December evening, I am walking along the fire road above Santa Ynez Canyon, looking for rain beetles. A movement in a patch of dead grass beside the road catches my eye and I stoop to see a dark, long-legged spider creeping this way and that, obviously looking for something. A little less than an inch long, with a tan abdomen, it must be a male trapdoor spider, hunting a female.

I shine my flashlight around his search area, though I know her door will be well camouflaged by bits of soil and debris spun into its surface. Something, perhaps her perfume, must be guiding him, for he takes the right step, a little door in the soil pops open, and a dark, shiny spider rushes out. She neither attacks nor resists when he crawls over her and plays with her front legs. Then she stands on her rear legs, facing him, and he inserts one of the foot-like appendages near his mouth, which carries his sperm, into the genital opening in her abdomen.

Finished, he crawls off and she turns to her burrow. But the lid has fallen shut while all this was going on and I watch her pick at it for some time without success. When she made it, she beveled it and lined it with silk, so it fits very tightly—too tightly, at this moment. Just as I start to help her, she manages to pry it up and slide under. Usually, when she captures passing prey, she keeps one foot in the door, and is not caught with her door down.

The grassy patches trapdoor spiders favor occur throughout the mountains and can cover broad areas where soils are heavy and the climate too hot and dry to support extensive crowns of trees. Valleys and other level spots that collect water, ideal for grasslands, are most common in the northwestern part of the Santa Monicas. Some people believe that grasslands were more widespread before the arrival of Europeans because of frequent burning by the California Indians.

Relative to most other flowering plants, grasses seem monotonous to me. They all look somewhat alike, and their flowers are tiny and colorless. Be that as it may, grasses, such as rice, wheat, and corn, support the human race, directly or indirectly, by feeding people and livestock.

Competition from annual grasses brought from the Mediterranean has left only relict stands of native, perennial bunchgrasses in the Santa Monicas. Ray Sauvajot, an ecologist with the National Park Service, has found them in La Jolla Valley and portions of Rancho Sierra Vista, for example. Where native bunchgrasses survive or where annual grasses have been burned off, spring wildflowers splash particularly colorful displays among the widely spaced bunchgrass tussocks.

The February night is cold and clear, and the constellation, Orion, glitters in a moonless, black sky. A female coyote sneaks under scrub oaks growing down the south-facing slope above Serrano Canyon. She is approaching her favorite hunting ground, the broad, open grassland in Serrano Valley, where she found many ground squirrels, young brush rabbits, and Audubon's cottontails last summer.

But the ground squirrels, the only mammals (other than some bats) that hibernate in the Santa Monicas, are safely ensconced in their underground burrows, and the rabbits that survived her forays and those of red-tailed hawks and great-horned owls have become wary. Carrying pups, she is very hungry, and it has been weeks since she caught live prey.

Her keen senses of hearing and smell tell her a rabbit is grazing downwind on the dried herbs beyond the shrubs. Catlike, she creeps closer, eyes, ears, muzzle focused on her target. By the faint shine of Sirius, the brilliant star in the Great Dog constellation, her light-sensitive eyes make out a cottontail, about 5 feet from the edge of the bushes.

More than a foot long, excluding its ears, the cottontail will make a good meal, and is close enough to reach in a bound. She pulls herself together and springs.

The rabbit utters a tiny scream.

She snaps its neck with a single bite and gives the limp body a couple of shakes for good measure. Then she rips the belly open and steam rises in the cold air. She begins eating, starting with the gut.

About a dozen years ago, she could have found a black-tailed jackrabbit, which would have made an even better feast, but home building and other developments have taken much of the open space the jacks need. These days she comes upon them relatively infrequently.

In March, oaks come into full bloom. On sunny days, their pollen makes drifts of gold against the dark woodland background. The sight is lovely, but the clouds of pollen make me miserable because of my allergies.

Wind pollinates oaks. The male flowers cluster on hanging threads to form catkins that in the slightest breeze, quiver and release pollen. Each tree bears thousands of catkins and produces great showers of it.

Native bunch grass, La Jolla Valley trail.

Coast live oak catkins, Nicholas Flat.

Red-capped bolete mushrooms, Topanga Canyon. (AR)

Great purple hairstreak butterfly.

Johnny jump-ups, Arroyo Sequit.

This bounty ensures the wind will blow some pollen to female flowers of another oak of the same kind, but accidents happen, and hybrids can result from fertilization between different species of oaks.

One March night in Malibu Creek State Park, a dusky-footed woodrat smells a mushroom in leaf litter under a coast live oak. She zeros in on it and starts devouring it with obvious relish. It is the fruiting body of a red-capped bolete, a fungus preferring the roots of oaks. The mushrooms attract woodrats and other small mammals that disperse the spores in their moist, nourishing scat.

The fungus that produced this mushroom is an elaborate network of branching filaments interacting with the roots of the oak to form a structure called a mycorrhiza, which means fungus root. The filaments excrete enzymes that convert root tissues to fungus food.

Gopher snake. (DS).

At the same time, the mycorrhiza expands root contact with the soil and increases uptake of water and minerals and, thus, the ability of the oak to survive drought. The fungal filaments also form clumps that hold water and soil around the roots, reducing surface run-off and improving root penetration. Without mycorrhizae, many plants are stunted and eventually die.

In the daytime, great purple hairstreak butterflies glint in the treetops, but from the path below I rarely see these large, elegant insects. The upperwings of males are iridescent, turquoise blue (not purple). Underneath the butterflies are downright gaudy, with brilliant, orange abdomens setting off satiny, charcoal-gray underwings, decorated with spots of scarlet, chrome yellow, and turquoise blue. Females are darker and both male and female have trailing, dark streaks and hairlike projections on the hind-wing, from which comes their common name, "hairstreak." On mistletoe, which their green larvae eat exclusively, they are almost invisible.

New growth appears on the oaks and saplings start pushing up from buried acorns. Deer, rabbits, and rodents, many carrying young, relish the young shoots. Even where cattle are not grazing, few saplings will survive to become mature trees.

A family of ten acorn woodpeckers, noisy and sleek, after a winter well-supplied with nuts, is busy raising seven young. The nestlings are common offspring of a pair of sisters with a male and his two sons. The nest is stashed in a cavity in a cottonwood, growing near the marsh at the edge of the pond at Nicholas Flat.

Males and females worked together to prepare the cavity, and, now, assisted by five offspring of previous years, cooperate in feeding the brood. Though the juveniles are sexually mature, they hang around with their parents rather than setting out to raise families of their own. Other kinds of birds occasionally make social arrangements like these, but acorn woodpeckers are unusual in the consistency with which they do so.

They become monogamous only when the acorn

pickings have been very poor. Then the juveniles depart. Do the parents kick the kids out or do they go off to seek their fortune? We don't know.

On a cool March morning, Louise Sakamoto and I are walking in a clearing through live-oak woodlands in Topanga State Park. "Oh, look! How pretty!" she says, pointing at a little patch of golden flowers borne on long stems above heart-shaped leaves.

"They're Johnny jump-ups," I say, getting my camera ready to take a picture.

"They look like tiny pansies."

"In the same family—the violets. They're the only ones native to the Santa Monicas." I kneel to the flowers. "Damn! Not much light." I slow the shutter speed and hold my breath.

"Did you get it?" Louise says when I straighten.

"I'll find out when it comes back from the developer."

"But, you know," I go on, "Johnny jump-ups are special beyond just being lovely. They're the only food for the caterpillars of Comstock's fritillary butterfly. I've never seen one, but their pictures are quite charming.

"As I remember it, Comstock said:

'When the grassy foothills have changed their verdant spring garb for the tan of late [spring], this spangled beauty comes forth to flaunt its lustrous wings in the bright sunlight. Always it seeks the haunts where . . . the yellow violets' earlier bloomed.

"As late as 1973, these fritillaries were abundant in the Santa Monicas, but now they're very rare."

"Because there aren't many violets?"

"Once there were sheets of them," I say, thinking of a passage in Rindge's book. "Too many people want to live where they do."

Walking farther, we discover a coast live oak with round balls on a few of its twigs. These are oak apples, formed where a live oak gall wasp has laid her eggs or wasp larvae have hatched. The galls, which turn reddish brown as summer progresses, feed and protect the developing larvae at the same time that they defend the tree against them.

Wasps emerging from oak apples are all fertile females, small and odd-looking, with greatly enlarged abdomens. They lay eggs that cause the oak to make mushroomlike galls (not apples) on its leaves. The leaf galls contain both male and female larvae. When mature, these mate to create the next generation of female wasps in oak apples.

Though a single tree may host as many as half a million wasps in one breeding season, biologists think the galls are not usually harmful to the oak. Also, oak apples can hang for a few years before dropping, so the presence of a lot of oak apples doesn't necessarily mean the tree is heavily infested. In autumn I've driven along the northern side of the Santa Monicas and seen oaks hung with so many oak apples the woodland looked like an apple orchard.

Besides putting on a show, oak apples feed other animals than gall wasps. Acorn woodpeckers dig larvae out of them, rodents eat those that have fallen, and parasitoid wasps lay eggs in them so that their larvae will eat the gall-wasp larvae.

In the sunshine of an early April morning, a ground squirrel sits on a stump overlooking the meadow in Charmlee Park. She came out of hibernation in mid-March and is fat from eating tender new leaves, flowers, and bulbs, as well as insects and small animals. Her burrow, which she shares with several other ground squirrels, is close by, under a rock beside the road, rather than in the meadow, where tall grass would block her view.

There has been a lot of rain this spring, and a

Oak apple.

Ground squirrel.

Western meadowlark. (MP)

heavy patch of wild oats hides a gopher snake sliding toward her. When her gaze shifts, he slithers a few more inches, holding his head high and moving it slightly from side to side to improve his depth perception. She hops down on the way to some black mustard and he is on her at once, folding her in the loops of his body, squeezing. Within a few minutes she dies of suffocation.

In the Santa Monica Mountains, only gopher snakes are more common than rattlesnakes, but I come across them less often. Gopher snakes spend most of their time underground looking for mice, rats, and other prey, whereas, since I hike in the early morning, I often find rattlesnakes stretched across the trail warming up.

One day in May, Mary Valentine shows me a common buckeye butterfly on the trail to La Jolla Valley. The distinctive eyespots, that look like the spots on the ends of peacock feathers, give the buckeye family its name, "peacock butterflies."

We see a plain, little common ringlet butterfly looking for grasses to deposit her eggs on. The buckeye (clearly a male, from his behavior) will have none of her. He flies up and gives her a few whacks with his

Brush rabbit. (LS)

White-crowned sparrow. (MP)

wings, driving her away from his stretch of path and the stand of California plantains, one of the food plants for buckeye larvae.

We watch him a while, hoping a receptive female will show up. It could be a pretty sight if she does, for the pair sometimes does a little dance, fluttering together into the blue sky and returning to the ground to mate. But not today. Instead, the buckeye starts chasing a red-winged grasshopper and flies off.

By the end of May, dried annual grasses cover open land with hues of beige and ochre. Three hundred years ago these patches would have been tinged with the green that persists at the base of perennial bunch grasses even when the tops and seed heads have dried.

June is hot and a mountain lion and her two kittens have been sleeping most of the day in their den on Brents Mountain above Malibu Creek. More than a week earlier, she had discovered her mate sniffing around the den and had given him a warning snarl. Fearing he would kill the kits if he found them unprotected, she moved them to a crevice on the south side of the mountain.

She has been feeding the family from a deer she

Comstock's fritillary butterfly. (JL)

Buckeye butterfly, Santa Ynez Canyon.

hid among the rocks in Udell Gorge. Last night, what little remained of the carcass had turned putrid and was swarming with maggots. She set off to make another kill, but the deer family had moved out. She had started to track them along a ledge when she looked down on a brush rabbit eating dry grasses, jumped on it, and carried it back to the kits. It would tide them over for a day.

Early the next evening, hungry and eager, she starts out, following pellets of deer scat up the east side of Udell Gorge toward Liberty Canyon. At one point she stops, depositing several large cylinders of scat, scraping the ground to mark her territory like a house cat.

She tops the ridge above the canyon and looks over a savanna containing groves of majestic valley oaks. Perhaps she sees the trees as beautiful, because in the past, she has found deer under them, browsing oak boughs that droop almost to the ground and eating leaves of poison oak, toyon, and coffeeberry that have grown up since cattle-grazing stopped.

These woodlands are between one hundred and three hundred years old and individual trees, some over 100 feet tall, may be as old as four hundred years. Their roots reach a permanent supply of deep water.

Deer-scent draws the lioness a half-mile up the

Burrowing owl. (LS)

canyon, where a family of four is feeding, enormous ears constantly turning to catch the sound of approaching predators. A quarter moon casts a faint light over trees and grasses and the lion, belly close to the ground, muscles rippling, creeps toward the deer through a path of shadows, sidling along rocks in the stream bottom, following a line of shrubs up the bank where the trees form a dark mass with glinting leaves. Her broad-padded feet make no sound as she places them on the stones, taking care not to dislodge any.

She freezes at a sudden rattle of pebbles and flurry of wings in her face. She has startled a burrowing owl that had been poised at the entrance of his home in the bank, readying himself for the night hunt.

The deer are startled, too, and though they do not see the lion, they play it safe, bounding away from the grove and into the dimly-lit grassland, where nothing can sneak up on them. She dashes at them, but they easily outrun her and she must continue her search elsewhere.

As the summer goes on, male ground squirrels become very fat and, by August, retire to their burrows to enter a state similar to hibernation and escape the summer heat. Female ground squirrels start

hibernating later, probably because nursing pups in the spring delay their own accumulation of fat.

In late September, migrating birds and winter visitors start arriving, looking for insect larvae, seeds, and ripe berries. Cedar waxwings are especially partial to mistletoe berries, whose sticky seeds they spread from oak to oak in their droppings. By October, the distinctive song of white-crowned sparrows is once again ringing over the dry grasses on the hill below Nicholas Flat. The white-crown nests where the winters are colder and comes to my mountains to eat seeds that ripened in summer. And western meadowlarks that nested farther north have joined meadowlarks that raised their young in southern California grasslands.

When the chill rains start the year again, birds and deer are enjoying the acorn harvest and female ground squirrels are safe in their underground nests.

Liberty Canyon.

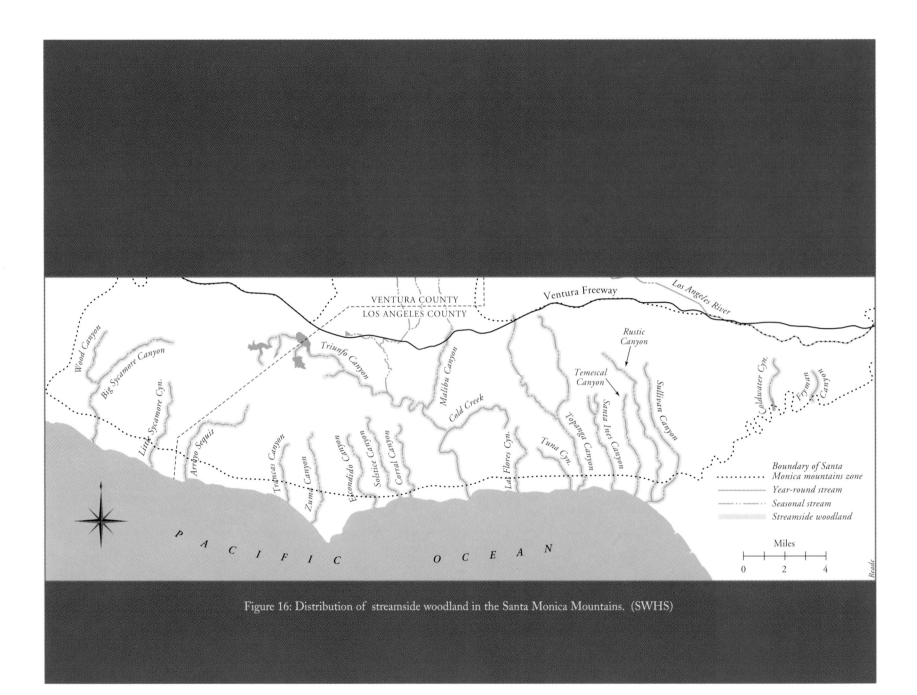

Figure 16: Distribution of streamside woodland in the Santa Monica Mountains. (SWHS)

CHAPTER 6

Fresh Water
—Shady Oases

LABORING UP A TRAIL ONE *JUNE* DAY, THROUGH THE CHAPARRAL IN *POINT* *MUGU* State Park, I hear the burble of running water below, and my hot, sweaty, dusty self yearns for it. Down I drop into cool shade beneath tall trees. There's a picnic table beside the stream, for I'm not the only person who loves a refreshing creek.

Fresh-water ecosystems cover less than 5 percent of my mountains, yet these ecosystems are essential, directly or indirectly, to many mountain animals and plants. Figure 16 shows major areas near natural fresh water. Solid lines designate the four streams that flow all the time regardless of rainfall. The others, which usually dry up in late summer and fall, are shown by dashed lines.

All of the freshwater lakes and ponds in the mountains are man-made. Since the time of the missions, people have dammed the streams to control winter floods and save rainwater for themselves and livestock, and, ultimately, for fun. Lakes and ponds not lined with cement, such as Upper Franklin Canyon Reservoir, Century Lake, and Malibu Lake,

have created ecosystems needing still, fresh water in the Santa Monicas.

On a November night, I am walking to my car from a friend's house in Monte Nido when I notice movement by the side of Cold Canyon Road. My flashlight catches little, lizardlike creatures glistening in the dampness left by an evening shower.

They're California newts, migrating toward their breeding pools from underground places where they've hidden away during the dry autumn. I look up at the night sky, clear, except for a few wisps of clouds, and wonder whether it's true that newts navigate by the stars.

Newts breathe through their lungs and skin and must have fresh water to breed and change from larvae into adults. For them, "fresh water" means water that's unpolluted and unsilted. My scientist friend, Lee Kats, has shown me much of the life in mountain streams. He says newts are among the most poisonous animals on the planet. In fact, newt tissue can kill most vertebrates, including man, if enough is eaten, so nothing preys on them except little boys,

Picnicing by Cold Creek.

California newt, Arroyo Sequit.

California bay tree in flower on Sandstone Peak.

who find them easy to catch. (The good professor, too, enjoys catching them, though not just for the fun of it.)

By December, white alders and sycamores have lost their leaves. Sun warms the streambed in Solstice Canyon where they grow, and bare wands of arroyo willow and red willow border the water. On streamside terraces, leaves of coast live oak provide a rich, green background for my hike up the creek.

Dainty bunches of yellow-green flowers already decorate the leafy branches of the California bay trees growing above the stream. During a cooler, wetter geological period, the Santa Monica Mountains had extensive forests of bays. Now they survive only in moist areas.

In Oregon, the bay is called myrtlewood, and the hard, swirl-grained wood is used to make decorative pieces. I use the pungent leaves to flavor stews and other dishes, though I have to take care not to overpower my production. The kitchen bay leaf has a milder flavor.

I stop to look at a mass of convergent ladybugs on a bare branch beside the trail. They've huddled together to keep warm, as honeybees do at this time of year, and will probably move under a rock or log as the cold deepens.

As I sit on the branch to take a closeup photograph, I think they would make a filling meal for birds or lizards if they did not, when threatened, secrete a bitter fluid that is probably poisonous to vertebrates. No doubt their orange-and-black pattern warns off potential enemies.

Of the more than a hundred species of ladybugs in California the convergent ladybug is the most common. In fact, it is one of the commonest California insects.

Dusk is coming to Solstice Canyon when I start back to my car, entertained by the krrreck-ek of Pacific treefrogs singing in chorus. What a lovely, liquid sound! No doubt they'll soon be breeding in the backwaters of the creek, where they gathered in November after emerging from their dry-season torpor. Farther inland where it's colder, they won't start to chorus until February.

The black mask through the eye of the adult treefrog identifies this species. (Despite their name, they don't live in trees.) They need water for the same purposes as do the newts, but are not as fussy about where they breed. Any place will do, even a roadside ditch, if water stays there long enough (four or five months) for tadpoles to hatch and turn into adult frogs.

My pictures of the ladybugs are still in my camera when I wake one morning, five days later, scratching the backs of my thighs. I look in the mirror and am aghast to see a fierce, red rash on both my legs.

Damn! Poison oak!

I must have sat on it, unknowing, to take the ladybug pictures. Like the alder and sycamore, poison oak is deciduous, and without its leaves I didn't recognize it.

I'm in for weeks of itching and oozing, because my years in the mountains have sensitized me to poison oak oil. Only a course of prednisone will stop such a severe reaction, which it does by suppressing my immune response.

Poison oak, which is easily identified by its leaves-in-three (let it be!), is not an oak, but a member of the sumac family. In a region of the U.S. where people pronounce sumac "shu-mac," a learned man pontificated that "sumac" and "sugar" were the only words in English where "su" was pronounced "shu."

Poison oak in bloom in Arroyo Sequit Canyon.

Pacific treefrog. (DS)

Bobcat. (NPS)

A listener asked, "Are you sure?"

One night, toward the end of January, a warbling yowl brings a woman living in Arroyo Sequit Canyon upright in her bed. "Puss-cat?" she says. But he is safe and warm on her feet, though his ears are twitching. The howl comes again and raises the hair on her scalp. She puts her head out the window and hears the wild cry rising from the canyon above the house.

Mountain lion, she thinks, with a thrill of fear, and pictures the sinuous, tawny cat. She makes sure her little girl is safe in bed, knowing that mountain lions sometimes attack children.

She has made a common error, for mountain lions are usually silent. What she has heard is a male bobcat serenading a female, who, in heat, has lured him with her perfume. He may have traveled as far as 20 miles to find her. To make sure he does, she has marked earth, rocks, and bushes with excrement and a fluid from her anal gland.

The bobcat's tail is so short it looks as though it has been bobbed off, hence the common name. Their elfin ear tufts are also unusual and contribute to bobcats' keen hearing, and their buff, mottled color helps them fade into their dry mountain surroundings.

Fortunately, bobcats, vital predators of rodents and rabbits, aren't rare in the Santa Monica Mountains. Therefore, there's little danger these two will be inbreeding. One reason for their abundance is

Ladybugs hibernating near Cold Creek.

Humboldt lily, Cold Creek.

their fertility—their litters can contain as many as six kits. In addition, if the first mating is infertile, they'll breed again.

During January and February, several storms saturate the ground and, in March, a four-day downpour swells mountain streams to roaring rivers. Doris Hoover, a botanist friend who is helping Solstice Canyon return to its natural state, watches in dismay as water scours out the soil from bank to bank, up to 4 feet above the normal creek bed. Giant oaks, alders, and sycamores tumble downstream, along with huge bundles of uprooted saplings, including native shrubs and trees Doris had planted. Mud and gravel pouring over the streambed bear an unseen cargo of invertebrates, eggs, and seeds to add to the burst of life when spring arrives.

By mid-March, twenty male newts are prowling the pond below the waterfall at Cold Creek, waiting for females to show up. Above the pool, a dainty Venus maidenhair fern grows out of the rock. Like other ferns and mosses, it needs a film of water, in which its sperm can swim to an egg. It often grows on calcium-rich seepages and rocks like the one over which the water is dropping.

Before the end of March, the first female newt slides innocently into the water, perhaps anticipating

Venus maidenhair fern on Cold Creek falls.

a gentle embrace. Immediately the males engulf her, forming an orgiastic ball of lust. A day or two later, they unwind, either to enfold another female or deposit packages of sperm on the pond bottom. Freed, at last, the female picks up a package with her cloaca and fertilizes her eggs.

Cold Creek is one of the least disturbed streamsides in the Santa Monicas, and, perhaps, in southern California. It is also unusual in that it's very small, yet never stops flowing. Even at the peak of the seven-year drought, water, essential for the vertebrates and invertebrates that live in it, trickled down the creekbed. Fortunately, the Mountains Restoration Trust currently protects Cold Creek from development and human disturbance.

In April, Mary Valentine shows me one of her favorite spots—a pond dug for watering cattle when Arroyo Sequit was a working ranch. "I can spend the whole day watching the pond," she says. "You could go crazy on aquatic insects."

She continues, "Last year it dried out and looked sterile. A lot of the pollywogs hadn't quite metamorphosed and they all died. One of the reasons it dries up so fast is because of all the gopher holes."

That's a disadvantage of man-made ponds, I think. Their water level fluctuates so much they can't

Mountain kingsnake, Cold Creek.

Green-backed heron. (BS)

California treefrog in Cold Creek.

maintain the ecosystem.

"After all the rains," she goes on, "the whole bottom of the pond was moving with water mites, tiny, eight-legged creatures that prey on and parasitize aquatic animals. We had lots of birds—towhees, scrub jays, mallards, green-backed herons, black phoebes. Now, there are all sorts of diving beetles, lots of spiders on the water, water striders, water boatmen. Some of the waterbugs fly into the pond after it fills. Birds bring others in on their feet. The insects burrow into the mud and survive until the rains come again."

Ah, the persistence of life, especially where water is available!

Down by Arroyo Sequit Creek, spectacular Humboldt lilies are blooming the day after May Day. Many of the nodding blossoms are at eye level or higher, where Jim and I can enjoy them and take pictures without stooping. The orange anthers dangle, loose on the ends of their stamens, ready to shower pollen on hummingbirds, orioles, and other nectar-sippers. Unfortunately, thoughtless people cut off the blossoms, depriving the plant of its chance to reproduce and multiply.

Mary takes me to the pond at Rocky Oaks in May. "It's fun to watch damselflies mate," she says, checking my expression to make sure I'm not offended. "The male puts his sperm in a little pouch he has and the female puts herself into the pouch and you'll see them flying around stuck together like that." The female's head is held at the tip of the male's abdomen.

"I like to watch them lay their eggs," she goes on. "Sometimes the male still has hold of the female but they're in a slightly different position than when they're mating. He may fly low and dip her abdomen in the water to wash off the eggs, or, depending on the species, she'll put the eggs on the stem of a plant coming out of the water."

"Once I watched yellowjackets eating a dragonfly just after it emerged from its molt, before its wings were hardened. They ate it from the bottom of its abdomen up."

Yes, aquatic insects are fascinating, sometimes in a horrible way.

A week later, I've scrambled down the bluff, into Las Flores Canyon, to look at spring flowers, and am admiring a tall stand of hummingbird sage when I give a start. A series of glistening red, black, and yellow bands is slithering along the rocks. If this were Arizona, it might be a highly venomous coral snake. But coral snakes don't live in my mountains, so I take a closer look and see the red bands are bordered by black, not yellow or white, as in a coral snake.

I'm thrilled. This is my first sighting in the wild of our very own harmless mountain kingsnake. Its scientific name ends in pulchra, to proclaim its exceptional pulchritude, and, indeed, it looks like an elegant, beaded belt.

Unlike its relative, the California kingsnake, it's too small to eat rattlesnakes, though it dearly loves lizards. It also needs cooler and moister areas, such as those along streams, and lives on the coastal side of the mountains and in the Malibu Creek drainage.

In June, Lee lifts a glistening, loose mass of Pacific treefrog eggs out of Cold Creek, and I smile to see tiny tadpoles pulling free of it. Even at this small

Ringtail.

scale, emergence of life delights me.

On a sandstone rock in the middle of the same stretch of stream, a California treefrog is basking. It is light mottled gray, the same color as the rock it sits on, with obvious toe pads and no distinctive markings, and can change color in a few minutes. I wave my hand within a foot of it, but it stays still, apparently assuming it can't be seen. If prey were to come close enough, however, it would strike.

California treefrogs like mountain freshets with lots of bedrock and boulders. They need undisturbed streams throughout their life cycles, while California newts and western toads must have them only for breeding and the larval or tadpole stage.

I meet Lee at Cold Creek again in late June, when the newts should be hatching. Sure enough, little, spotted, big-eyed larvae with external, feathery gills hanging on the sides of their heads are swimming in the shallows. He says they like these areas, where the sun keeps them warm.

Their main predators are toe-biters (giant waterbugs) and, appallingly (to people), adult newts. Sure enough, several adults are still in the pool below the waterfall. They haven't gone back into the hills after breeding, as the field guides say they do.

They eat whatever is alive, including crane fly

larvae and caterpillars that fall into the stream as well as their own young, as the professor and his students have shown. Why this is happening is an enigma. In fact, adult newts emit chemical cues that should scare newt larvae into hiding.

Buttonlike shadows skitter on the bottom of a clear, still pool created by a partial dam in Cold Creek. Dimples in the surface, around the feet of common water striders, cast the shadows as the insects look for prey above and below the water. They mate year round, communicating their intentions by making ripples in the surface film.

By July, in Solstice Canyon, the broadened, clean, sandy floodplain opened by last winter's floods is sprouting willow shoots, sedges, weeds, and scarlet monkeyflower. Inch-high saplings of sycamore and alder rise among the streambed cobbles, while, where they survived the spring flood on higher, shaded banks, live oak seedlings are 3 to 5 feet tall.

A female ringtail "cat" that has been snoozing away a hot August day wakes in the late evening in her den near Garapito Creek. Lying in her bed of leaves, she grooms herself, like a cat, licking her fur and cleaning her ears, cheeks, and nose with moistened forepaws. Her three kittens are in the nest with her, though she and her mate have been feeding them brush mice and other small prey since early July.

Frontier miners considered ringtails better mousers than domestic cats and kept them in mines to control rodents. Despite their catlike looks and behavior, they are not cats, but closely related to raccoons and pandas. Uncommon in the Santa Monicas, ringtails are seldom seen, not only because of their scarcity but because, like many wild mammals, they are almost completely nocturnal.

After her bath, the ringtail sets out refreshed and ready for the hunt. In the small hours of the night, having caught enough rodents for herself and her kittens, she starts back to the den. Within a few hundred feet of it, a bobcat leaps on her from a boulder along the game trail.

Fortunately, the cat's pounce is slightly off the mark. The ringtail drops the rats she is carrying and jumps free, screaming and squirting a foul-smelling fluid from her anal gland. The bobcat backs off, distracted from the rats. It is not that desperate for a meal. The ringtail's ability to eject a stinking scent earned it another name, "civet cat," referring to the African animal that produces the musk used in perfumes.

In September, Jim and I are sitting under a willow along the bank at Malibu Creek State Park, having a picnic of fruit, roasted chicken, iced tea, and chocolate chip cookies. I sense a stealthy movement in the shadows along the shore, but see nothing.

"Look, a green-backed heron," he says.

I look where his binoculars are trained and see a long, yellow-green foot carefully rise, hesitate, carefully settle into the water without a ripple.

"It's got something in its beak," he says. "Looks like a feather."

"What's it doing?" I say. The small, chunky bird is moving the feather back and forth over the water.

With a flash, a fish rises to the lure, the heron grabs the fish and proceeds to swallow it.

"Amazing," he says. "I never saw that before!"

That was our last outing before the rains arrived.

Mugu Lagoon and environment.

CHAPTER 7

By the Sea

WHEN I LOOK OUT AT THE OCEAN MY SOUL EXPANDS INTO VASTNESS, stretched by the horizon to what seems an unmeasurable distance. The Channel Islands are misty shapes along the edge of the world. Many times I have lost myself to the open, sighing, gray-blue waters, my face bathed by moist, salt air carrying faintly oily scents, my bare feet cooled by foam advancing, retreating, advancing, retreating—my busy thoughts washed away.

From Santa Monica Canyon to Point Mugu, the Santa Monica Mountains rise directly from the ocean and, surely, the sea is integral to the mountains if only because of its profound effects on climate. Figure 3 shows coastal areas bordering the mountains and notes some of the beaches set aside for public enjoyment.

To me, as to many, thoughts of the sea first bring images of the strand and sunbathing, swimming and picnicking. But some people soon discover other treasures. In winter, strings of birds, like sanderlings and willets, mesmerize us as they scamper in and out along wave edges, probing for molluscs, crabs, and worms. In the waters beyond the surf, schools of fish draw fishermen and western gulls, brown pelicans, surf scoters, and other sea ducks.

On an early Monday morning in October, the sky is clear and a light breeze wafts cool air over the sparkling sand of Topanga Beach. More than a dozen ring-billed gulls strut, cry, and jostle around a trash barrel overflowing with leftovers from Sunday picnickers. A week ago, these birds arrived in Santa Monica Bay for their winter vacation. The adults have bred and fledged their offspring in south-central Canada. Along the coast, the natural year begins with the arrival of large numbers of water-loving birds rather than the rains.

Six California gulls and two western gulls mix in. The California gulls nested with the ring-bills in the summer just past, but the westerns raised their young on the Channel Islands. One big western shoves aside a ring-billed pecking a leftover turkey sandwich, well-dusted with sand. The other western swoops at a California trying to fly off with a half-eaten chicken wing and makes the smaller gull drop his treasure.

Birding at Malibu Lagoon.

Harbor seals. (MP)

Mugu Rock.

Just before dawn, the last Sunday before Christmas, Jim and I drive up PCH, heater on and wipers flopping. When we get out in the Malibu Lagoon parking lot, wet ocean air makes our cheeks tingle. Gray shapes materialize in the cold dawn light on the lagoon, and we start trotting down the nature trail, spotting scope jouncing on Jim's shoulder. The situation is very different from our outings with other birders earlier in the year, when many of us had bare legs and arms.

We're off on the Audubon Society annual Christmas Bird Count. During two weeks, including Christmas and New Year, birders all over America are hoping to see lots of species of birds and to tally many birds of each species. Larry Allen, head honcho for the Malibu count, has kindly agreed to let us do the areas around the lagoon, the richest in L.A. for birds.

We work so hard all morning, we almost forget to meet the other birders for lunch at Tapia Park. There, our report of having seen an osprey and an unusual duck, a so-called "common" goldeneye, lures a couple of other birders to go back to Malibu with us. By that time, the goldeneye has disappeared but the tide has gone out and small flocks of shorebirds have arrived to feed on exposed flats.

At day's end, when there's too little light to see, we meet the rest of the L.A. contingent to go over our lists and fill up on pizza and beer. Larry is ebullient and assures us our total of 169 species will be among the top twenty, continentwide. So what if we have wind-burned cheeks and sore feet!

On a blustery February afternoon, I watch more than a hundred harbor seals hauled out north of the mouth of Mugu Lagoon under a sun glittering in a gray sky. Unlike California sea lions, which bark almost continuously, they are silent except for a rare, loud, snuffle, snort or groan, as they recharge their stores of oxygen. Mottled olive-brown, unmoving, they look like enormous hunks of scat deposited on the muddy bank.

At this time of year, most females are carrying pups, the result of mating nearly a year earlier. The single, fertilized egg was implanted in the uterine wall only a few months ago so that births are spaced about a year apart.

Because peoples' presence easily disturbs harbor seals, and to protect the females from miscarrying, the Navy has prohibited entry to the opposite beach, on the bank of which I'm watching the seals. A prominent sign announces the prohibition.

Chilled by a cold wind, I go back to my car and am ready to leave when two men of Japanese descent drive up in a van and park beside me. They pull on hip-high, rubber waders and start toward the lagoon, carrying fishing tackle. Surprised, I wait, wondering whether they've planned to disobey the Navy's injunction. A few minutes later, they return, get in the van and drive off. If this area were under civilian control, I think, some people would have flouted the order.

I have permission to explore the lagoon, off-limits to the general public in 1994. Originally, the Navy shut the public out of Mugu Naval Air Weapons Station, which surrounds the lagoon, to protect military security and air space for takeoffs and landings. Of late, the Navy has also protected the eastern arm of the lagoon as an ecological reserve, and Naval con-

Peregrine falcon. (MP)

trol has continued to limit human disturbance in the remainder. As a result, people see little of Mugu from the highway besides Mugu Rock, which is actually a notch the road builders left in the mountain.

One afternoon, when the sun is glaring through a thin overcast on tidal ponds east of the runway, a

Sea lettuce, Malibu Lagoon.

Tide pool, Malibu Lagoon.

Fixed snails, Malibu Lagoon.

peregrine falcon scans flocks of shorebirds and ducks from a high tower. Her jutting, charcoal-gray brows and cheek-patches soak up reflections around dark, liquid eyes as she searches for likely targets. High tide has bunched the birds in shallower water.

She lifts her tail, excretes, takes off and, with rapid beats of pointed wings, circles above the tower, gaining altitude with each loop. She has spotted a small duck, well apart from other birds, on a pond nearly a quarter-mile inland, so far away the image shimmers. At about 500 feet, she levels off and flies toward the bird, whose head is under water much of the time as it searches for crustacea.

When she is nearly over the duck, which is a green-winged teal, she pitches down, speeds her descent with a few quick wing beats, pulls wings close to body to become bullet-shaped, and dives at more than a 150 miles an hour. One writer has likened the peregrine to "a meteor in feathers."

Too late, the teal glimpses its attacker and, as it struggles into the air, the falcon strikes its head with a clenched foot and knocks it out with a single blow. She grasps her prey with long, sickle-shaped talons (for which falcons are named) and neatly severs its neckbone in the notch at the end of her bill.

The kill would surely have thrilled noble gentlemen who used peregrines for hunting in the Middle Ages. Does it give the bird a similar thrill?

With the duck in her claws, she heads back to her perch. Tom Keeney, the Navy's Ecologist and Natural Resource Manager at Mugu, reports that peregrines nest on the Northern Channel Islands, a hopeful sign for the birds. Twenty years ago, pesticides had nearly wiped them out and they are still rare.

In winter, they have plenty of incentive to make the flight across the channel. Tom says that at any time between November and May, upwards of 15,000 water-loving birds are on the 2,600 acres of lagoon, tidal creeks and ponds, mud and sand flats and marshes, feasting on rich supplies of fish, crustacea, molluscs and worms.

In March at low tide, I visit tidepools at the mouth of Malibu Lagoon with Pat Enkema, professor emeritus of biology at L.A. Pierce College. It's best to explore the pools when the tide is out far enough to expose the lowest zone and uncover the most animals and plants.

As we walk toward the water, Pat says, "Think small. Most of the animals here are tiny or even microscopic."

We squish about, tennis shoes protecting our feet from rocks and barnacles. Pat explains that the lovely, apple-green, frilly, leaflike growths waving in the water are sea lettuce, an alga ("alga" is singular for "algae"). Crabs are browsing it, snipping it off with their pincers and passing it to their mouths. It's so nutritious that in many countries people eat it.

Algae are true plants, but, unlike most land plants, lack specialized tissues for moving materials, such as sap, throughout the plant body. They produce most of the food in the tidal zone and are a refuge or home for many kinds of animals. They have cellulose cell walls similar to those found in green land plants, of which they may be the ancestors.

"What're these, Pat?" I say, pointing to a cluster of limey, ridged tubes twined about one another. "Worm shells?"

"Oh, those are special," she says. "They're actually snails. But don't be embarrassed. Even trained zoologists have thought they were worm shells. Each tube is the shell of a fixed snail that's grown around its buddies."

"What's making that film above them," I say. "Their excretions?"

"We're in luck!" Pat says. "Watch it a few minutes."

I sit on some rocks to wait, listening to the surf and noticing the chill seeping up my legs. After a minute or two, I say, "The film's getting darker and bits of things are catching in it."

"Right. It's a net of mucus the snails float up to catch food."

Suddenly, the film and its cargo disappears.

"See?" she says. "They sucked it in and now they're eating the whole thing."

Seawater has lots of decaying organic matter and dissolved minerals as well as a host of living, microscopic animals and plants (plankton). A similar wealth of nourishment is on, and buried in, the ocean bottom. In tidepools and on the bottom, anywhere there's something solid to attach to or burrow into, most of the animals live as anchored organisms, straining water and sand for food and oxygen.

Pat and I continue tidepooling, turning stones over to expose creatures living underneath and replacing them so we won't kill what would dry out or can't move quickly enough to escape predators. We find lots of little worms, crustaceans, and snails tucked into cracks and crannies. Think small, indeed!

Tidepools are the most demanding ecosystems in the whole ocean. Tidepool dwellers must cope with periodic heating and drying, wave shock and flooding with fresh water, which kills those that can't shut it out. Often sediment washes over or settles on tidepool dwellers, clogging their filters and smothering them. And they are prey to fish, birds, and land animals, including people. Many people allow their children to collect colorful starfish and other tidepool life, which is both illegal and extremely destructive of the ecosystem.

On the other hand, tidepools are also the richest ecosystems in the ocean. They are shallow enough to expose plants such as sea lettuce to the sunlight that promotes their growth and supplies food for animals that live in and on them. Also, abundant food washes into them from both land and sea.

One March morning at low tide, I walk out on the mud flats along Mugu Lagoon. At every step, water oozes and bubbles from holes and cracks in the mud as far as a foot or more from my boot. Obviously, burrows of various kinds of molluscs, worms, and crustaceans riddle the substrate.

On the flats along tidal creeks, large numbers of California hornsnails are grazing on fine, organic debris and single-celled algae coating the mud. Marshes often host more than a thousand hornsnails per square yard.

A long-billed dowitcher, a medium-sized member of the sandpiper family, is picking shorecrabs out of their shells. At the same time, several hornsnails are releasing larvae of parasitic worms, some of which the crabs eat. The dowitcher swallows these along with the crab meat. Inside the bird, they grow to adult worms and begin producing eggs. The dowitcher will excrete the eggs onto the mud, to be eaten by hornsnails, in which they will hatch into larvae, to start the cycle again.

In April on the salt marsh on the eastern arm of Mugu Lagoon, a shorebird, a male marbled godwit probes the mud for worms and crustaceans. His 4-1/2 inch, slightly upturned, pink bill with a black tip, makes him easy to spot among the other waders. He's getting ready for his flight to central Canada, where

Hornsnails on mud flats.

Marbled godwit. (DS)

Ghost shrimp. (DS)

Purple olive snail shells.

he'll breed in May, and his chest and belly are already turning a rich, tawny brown, with black barring.

With his long legs and bill, he can wade in deeper water and go after creatures that burrow at greater depths than can smaller shorebirds like dowitchers and western sandpipers. Many kinds of shorebirds may feed at the same time, on some of the same prey, but their different feeding methods (probing, pecking, sifting) and bill lengths allow them to exploit different prey assemblages.

The godwit plunges his head under water and, with sensitive nerves in his bill tip, feels a ghost shrimp, buried 5 inches in the mud, nabs it, works it up his bill and swallows it.

As soon as the godwit's bill jabs into the shrimp's burrow, a bump disappears from the burrow wall. It's the siphon of a clam, a California glass mya that's been sharing plankton and organic detritus swept

Pickleweed, Point Mugu.

Beach primrose.

into the burrow by the shrimp's breathing.

Without incessant excavation by the ghost shrimp, the burrow will soon disintegrate. Then the glass mya, which always lives near somebody's burrow, will have to find another protected spot for its siphon, or have a fish nip it off.

Of the twenty kinds of fish that depend on Mugu Lagoon for food and shelter, eight, including topsmelt, California halibut, and diamond turbot deposit eggs (spawn) in the lagoon and shiner surfperch use it for a nursery. California Indians ate California halibut, which, with diamond turbot and shiner surfperch are commercially valuable today.

Fish spawning begins in April, which is also when Tom Keeney starts monitoring the status of Mugu's breeding population of snowy plovers. Within the last few years, biologists have become concerned with the decline in snowy plovers because

of disturbance of nesting grounds. He says that the numbers of several other birds breeding in and around the lagoon have fallen precipitously: Belding's savanna sparrow, California least tern, and light-footed clapper rail. This is hardly surprising, since southern California wetlands, of which Mugu Lagoon and Malibu Lagoon are remnants, are also in short supply.

While he surveys the eastern arm of the lagoon, I tag along to take pictures of sand verbena and beach primrose in bloom. He is soon out of view and I stop now and then to pop the ball-shaped floats that suspend the blades of giant perennial kelp, whose remains litter the beach. This spectacular plant is the best-known of all the algae. Beach-goers often see its

olive-brown stalks lying on the sand like piles of ropes. The word "giant" is well chosen, as these plants typically grow to 200 feet or longer and form kelp forests that shelter and feed many kinds of fish and other animals. Kelp is also a major source of algin, a substance used in thickening foods and smoothing sauces.

On the sand, I find a beautifully shaped, lavender-tinged shell of a purple olive snail. The snail's habit of plowing along just under the surface of the sand has polished the shell to a high gloss and it's clear why California Indians treasured the shells and used them for trade and decoration.

During a low tide in May, Pat Enkema and I

come upon two sea hares in Malibu Lagoon, one about 10 inches long, the other somewhat smaller, joined at each end. They're mating, each acting as both male and female at the same time. Every sea hare has both testes and ovaries, and male and female genitalia, and can play either role, or both at once.

Most people who putter around in tidepools have amused themselves by poking sea hares to see them surround themselves with clouds of lovely, deep purple. The animal, a strict vegetarian, makes ink from pigments in the algae it eats. Predators dislike both the ink and parts of the sea hare itself. As do Pat and I, for sticky mucus covers it and leaves purple blobs on our hands. It's a kid's quintessence of grossness.

A few weeks later in a rocky pool, each of our sea hares will extrude long, spaghettilike, yellow strings of eggs forming a mass as big as a grapefruit. I do mean "mass," for it will contain tens of millions of eggs, of which a sea hare may lay half a billion during the season.

Thank heaven sea hares cannot fertilize themselves! Still, with nothing eating adult sea hares and each laying up to half a billion eggs, for a moment Pat and I envision a world engulfed in sticky, sluglike blobs. Fortunately, clams, and other creatures that eat plankton, ingest sea-hare larvae by the jillion, so this nightmare won't become reality.

With a high-pitched whine, a resin bee zips over foot-tall plants among saltgrass and pickleweed near the westernmost corner of Mugu Naval Air Station. She is visiting blossoms of the salt marsh bird's beak, an endangered plant, and is one of its most effective pollinators. She pushes her head and part of her thorax into the flower tube to probe to its base. In so doing, she picks up pollen, which she brushes onto the stigma of the next flower when she enters it.

She is a solitary bee and must rely on herself, alone, to perpetuate her kind. In her case, she has become bound to this stand of salt marsh bird's beak, as the better way to provide for her young in the short time she has.

The salt marsh bird's beak is an annual, partly parasitic on the roots of saltgrass and pickleweed, both of which flourish on salty soils. On the other hand, the bird's beak can't tolerate very salty soil and needs some fresh water to germinate. Thus, it needs soil whose saltiness changes too much for most other plants and grows only along a narrow band of salt marshes.

Pickleweed uses several strategies to thrive in salty soil. It is very succulent and stores water in its stems and branches. To decrease evaporation, its surface area is as small as possible, so its leaves look like rows of gray-green pickles, attached end to end, and its flowers are tiny little fringes set in the leaf joints. The plant stores the salt its roots take up, in the top pickles. In the fall, these turn red and fall off, ridding the plant of excess salt.

With autumn come the Santa Ana winds that push surface coastal waters out to sea. Colder, deeper layers, loaded with nutrients, well up to replace them and anchovies school there to feed. That's why brown pelicans and cormorants often gather near shore after Santa Anas blow.

One late October afternoon as I drive along PCH I look up at a line of gulls, snowy white against a brilliant, blue sky, sun glinting when outspread wings tilt in the breeze climbing the palisades. They're probably ring-bills, I think, though I can't stop on the highway to make sure. Thus, the natural year starts again along the coast of southern California.

Brown sea hare.

Humaliwo in winter. (JVZM)

CHAPTER *8*

California Indians
— The First Pioneers

OR AT LEAST *10,000* YEARS PEOPLE HAVE LIVED IN SOUTHERN CALIFORNIA. Throughout that time, they have altered the environment in ways we are just beginning to understand. In fact, before Europeans called a halt to Indian practices, they were changing the marine life, plants, animals, and the very landscape they lived in. They didn't merely pluck resources from the land, as I had imagined hunter-gatherers doing. Instead, they used a variety of methods to increase the productivity of the environment, as do most of the world's peoples who do not mass-produce food or goods.

Groups of Indians living in California were very different from one another, particularly with regard to language and religious beliefs. Kroeber, one of the first to study Native Californians in depth, identified more than one hundred separate tongues spoken in California. Around the Santa Monica Mountains, California Indians spoke languages and dialects derived from two language families.

To the north and west were people we call "Chumash"; the Spanish called people to the south and east of the Santa Monicas "Gabrielinos" and those due north "Fernandeños."

These groupings weren't what we think of as tribes, however. Most villages within these areas were politically independent of one another and the names the people had for themselves, which have largely been lost, came from the villages they lived in, as we in L.A. often call ourselves "Angelenos."

Indians living on the southern California coast from Malibu to Point Conception identified Santa Cruz Island as *Michumash*. In the early 1900s, anthropologists applied this name as *Chumash* to everyone from Malibu and the northern Channel Islands to San Luis Obispo.

The Indian name probably came from the word *'alchum*, meaning money. (The ' indicates a glottal stop, such as we use when we say "uh-oh.") People on the northern Channel Islands manufactured money, mostly from olivella shells. About a thousand years ago, they, and Indians living along the coast opposite the islands, developed an economy using olivella shell beads for money. By supplying most of the money

Olivella shell beads.

used in southern California, these people became one of the wealthiest California Indians.

For convenience only, I refer to California Indians living in the San Fernando Valley as Fernandeños and in the L.A. Basin as Gabrielinos. Among these people were groups called "Tongva," "Tobikhar," "Komiivat," and "Kizh," but we have no

"the place of." We think Topanga marks the western edge of Gabrielino settlement but all such borders fluctuated with time.

People making up the Gabrielinos-Fernandeños migrated west from the Great Basin to the coast of southern California between 500 B.C. and A.D. 1000. Around the Santa Monica Mountains they

Figure 17: Historic California Indian villages around and in the Santa Monica Mountains.

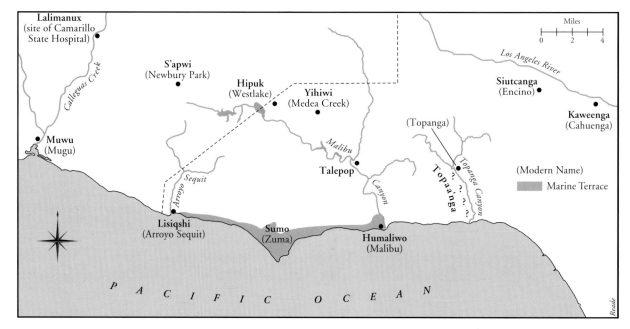

term referring to them as a whole other than the Spanish names.

They differed from the Chumash in several respects. Most importantly, their languages derived from Takic, or Shoshonean, whereas linguists classify the Chumash languages as Hokan. Some names of Takic origin are Kaweenga (Cahuenga) and Topaa'nga (Topanga), with the "nga" ending meaning

pushed aside the Hokan-speakers, who may have been here since 6000 B.C.

Except for religious beliefs, the newcomers quickly adopted much of the Chumash way of life. Life was easy in the L.A. Basin and San Fernando Valley, and these Indians became nearly as wealthy as their Chumash neighbors.

Figure 17 shows Indian villages whose locations

Abalone shell.

Mortar and pestle for grinding paint. (SU)

appear in the written record. Only Talepop was definitely interior to the mountains. In the northeast corner of Malibu Creek State Park, it was close to the trade route along Malibu Creek that connected the San Fernando Valley with the coast. The Spanish spelled the name *Tal'o'pop,* which is more accurate than the present-day spelling.

The location of *Topaa'nga* is less certain. It could have been in the mountains or near the mouth of Topanga Creek, or the name could have referred to the entire canyon.

The rugged Santa Monicas, with their cover of dense chaparral, hampered Spanish incursion into eastern Chumash territory, but no mountains defended the valley-dwelling Gabrielinos and Fernandeños. The Spanish immediately appreciated the value of the San Fernando Valley and the L.A. Basin for mission-ization and settlement. In fewer than a hundred years, they, Mexican, and later American settlers had almost eradicated the language and culture of these Indians and had nearly driven the people to extinction. Even so, early explorers and twentieth- century anthropologists have documented much of the Gabrielino-Fernandeño culture, along with that of the Chumash, some of whom have survived to the present.

As in the preceding chapters, my tales follow the seasons, but they shift across the millennia and among Indian groups and locations around the

Mortar and Pestle.

Santa Monicas.

I begin in December, when almost everyone was staying inside, out of the cold, rainy weather. The year can be any time going back a thousand years or more before the present. At the time, some thirty families were living in *Humaliwo,* a village on a terrace near present-day Malibu Lagoon. The painting recreates what the village might have looked like during the winter.

❦

Inside one of the houses, light from a small fire flickers on the broad faces and straight, black hair of a family that has just finished the evening meal. Besides the wife and husband, the group includes several family members who need, or simply enjoy, sharing daily work and play. In this case, they are the wife's widowed mother and sister, the couple's two married daughters, one holding a nursing infant, the daughters' husbands, and the couple's three unmarried sons and two unmarried daughters. The female side determines the lines of descent for this, and many, Chumash families.

The women's bare breasts and abalone shell necklaces gleam as they settle around the fire and the clicking of the shells and pretty stones decorating their two-piece deerskin skirts make a pleasant background to their soft talk. They also wear rabbit-fur capes to keep warm.

The husband wears only a waist-long sea-otter cape and the other men and younger girl, who hasn't reached puberty, are completely naked. The children sit behind their elders, who have the right to the best places by the fire.

The evening meal began with a starchy soup

made of atole, *or ground, leached acorns. The wife had worked throughout the day, first pounding just enough dried acorns, stored in a water-tight basket set on a platform inside the house, and then putting the flour in a sieve-like basket and running water through it to leach out the tannin. Then she cooked it with heated stones dropped in a water-tight basket. Next, the women had served dried elderberries, roast rabbit, and* pinole *cakes made of chia flour.*

The smoke-hole is shut to keep the rain out, so smoke hangs beneath the circular roof and seeps out around willow poles and through tule *(bullrush) thatch, killing any insects lodged there. One of the boys rubs his smarting eyes but says nothing.*

Odors of smoke and roast rabbit fill the house, but not the odor of unwashed bodies. Everyone had bathed before dawn that morning, as everyone does every morning.

The widow, Mut (her name means cormorant, a fishing bird), nods and everyone falls silent. Trained from girlhood to repeat Chumash myths and other stories word-for-word, she is a fine storyteller.

She begins:
Ever since September, Sun has been going farther and farther away from Earth and spending more and more time in His house in the world above this one.

The adults murmur assent and Mut nods, the abalone-shell discs on her necklace winking in the firelight.

She continues:
Every night of the year, Sun and Sky Coyote play a gambling game with a spinning top, staying up till dawn. There are two sides, with Sun and Eagle on one side and Morning Star (Venus) and Sky Coyote (the North Star) on the other. Moon is referee.

The wife and one of her daughters-in-law exchange smiles, for they both love to gamble and never tire of hearing how the Sky People enjoy it, too.

Mut says:
Sky Coyote watches over us from the sky. He works for us, gives us food, spares our lives. He looks like a big coyote.

Every evening when Sun returns home, he takes along whatever people he wants. He passes the people through the fire two or three times and then eats them half-cooked. He doesn't drink water, but blood. Every *day Sun carries off people from this world this way—every day.*

Mut pauses for a long time and looks around, but no one is impatient. Even the youngsters have seen people die and taken part in funeral rites.

Then Mut says:
Next week, the game between Sun and Sky Coyote will end and the players will count up who wins.

The listeners know the reckoning comes on the eve of the winter solstice, the time in December when the number of hours of daily sunlight stop decreasing and begin to increase. For the Chumash, as for many peoples who live by the seasons, the new year starts at the winter solstice.

Sun stakes all kinds of food on the outcome of the game—acorns, deer, holly-leaf cherry, chia, ducks and geese. If Sky Coyote's side wins, he can't wait to be paid but pulls open the door of the gaming house and Sun's stakes fall down into the world. But if Sun wins, He keeps His stakes and is paid in human lives.

That is, if Sky Coyote wins, rain will bring food to the people but, if Sun wins, there will be drought.

Scarcity of water must have limited the numbers of Indians living in southern California. It's ironic that today Angelenos complain when prolonged drought forces them to stop watering their lawns.

In my next tale, the Gabrielinos and Fernandeños probably didn't tell the story of Sun and Sky Coyote. Though they appropriated almost all Chumash material culture, their beliefs remained very different. For them, *Chengiichngech* was the supreme being, an ordinary man risen to heaven to become a supernatural, angry god who demanded an eye for an eye.

Thus, Shining Shell and her friends, Fernandeños who live in the San Fernando Valley, would have believed in *Chengiichngech.*

In March they are strolling together in the fields north of the mountain we call Ladyface, enjoying the fresh sunshine, watching old women and common folk dig mariposa lily bulbs, giggling when a startled rabbit scoots off.

The hillside is covered with sprouting bunchgrass, bulbs, chia, and other forbs. Last fall, the ladies watched the old women set fire to this grassland so it would grow lush and green this spring.

They have painted themselves with a thick coat of iron-rich earth to guard against sunburn. Now and then one of them bends down to pull up a handful of green shoots, which they call "little hair" and munch with relish. They taste mighty good after a winter spent eating dried food.

Shining Shell comes from a wealthy family in the village of Yihiwi, near what we call Medea Creek. She does very little of the work the other women do because her family owns the land and receives payment from the people they allow to gather food on it. If someone who shouldn't be there poaches on the land, a quarrel or even warfare may result. Her family's mark, concentric circles representing Sun, is painted on rocks, trees, and posts marking the boundaries of their land.

❦

The next story takes place at Muwu on a July morning, a thousand years earlier.

❦

Tomol. (SBMNH)

Sumiwowo, a Chumash, sees pelicans and cormorants circling and diving far out to sea.

"The bonito (skipjack) have come," he says, for he knows the birds are after squid and small fish, which the skipjack have driven to the surface. He has learned the ways of fish and other animals of the sea from his father, who was, like himself, captain of a sea-going canoe, or tomol. [The tomol in the photograph is a reconstruction now at the Santa Barbara Museum of Natural History.]

Sumiwowo is a member of the Brotherhood of the Tomol, a high-status, Chumash craft guild. His father traced his knowledge to Sulupiauset, the first man to make a tomol in modern form. Sulupiauset's tomols were so much better than the old ones the Chumash named the month of October in his honor.

Tomols are made from planks lashed together and sealed with asphaltum that oozes from the ground in southern California. Like many Chumash tomols, Sumiwowo's is made of redwood, which is very light and durable. A few months ago, four redwood logs washed up on the beach near Muwu.

At dawn the next morning, Sumiwowo and five other men from Muwu, a village of more than 200 people, set off in Sumiwowo's boat. Besides the men, the tomol carries drag nets with a large, 4-inch mesh as well as a boy to bail the water that will leak in throughout the trip. When they glide out from the beach, three other tomols slip into the water nearby.

Sumiwowo fingers his fishing talisman in a mesh bag on his belt, a tomol effigy made from steatite. Everyone is very excited. The men love the challenge of working together, the pride they feel when they pull their laden tomols onto the beach and the villagers admire their haul. And fresh fish will be a welcome addition to their recent diet of shellfish. Sumiwowo can almost taste it.

After less than an hour of paddling, the boatmen reach the place where the birds are swirling. Sumiwowo begins staring intently into the clear, dark water, looking for flashes of silver. Just when he's beginning to worry that the skipjack won't appear, a man in a nearby boat shouts and points.

Yes! There they are! A river of striped silver running beside the boats!

The boatmen stand, balancing carefully, and cast the nets behind. Then they paddle ahead, dragging the nets through the huge school of fish. In a few minutes, the nets are heavy with the catch and the boatmen begin hauling them in.

Sumiwowo exults, for his tomol is full of wet nets and beautiful, squirming fish. He is watching men in one of the other boats dragging a heavy load over the side when, without warning, the boat rolls toward the net and turns over, tossing men, net, and fish into the sea. The men quickly surface and start swimming toward their tomol, which is beginning to sink. The net with its fish has disappeared below.

Sumiwowo reaches for his talisman and discovers, to his horror, that it has fallen out of its bag into the mass of fish.

A gray whale heaves into sight, blowing a spout of mist into the air. It's like the whales the magic swordfish throw onto the beach now and then for the people of Muwu to feast on, but this time the whale has destroyed a whole netful of fish and threatened to drown people or sink the tomol, at the least.

The boatmen in the other tomols paddle to the swamped craft, pull the swimmers aboard and fasten the tomol behind Sumiwowo's, the biggest and strongest.

Sumiwowo is quiet as they make their way back to Muwu. The people of the sea had taken his talisman from him. Perhaps the shaman will give him a drink made from momoy, *so he can enlist his dream helper, Grizzly Bear, to counterbalance their power. He must not go to sea again until he has done this.*

We call momoy, *a common, poisonous member of the tobacco family, "jimson weed" or "datura." Only a shaman knows how to brew a nonlethal concoction from it and sometimes even a shaman's brew kills someone. As a rite of passage, all Chumash youngsters drink it to induce visions of the spirit world. While they're unconscious, sometimes for as long as twenty-four hours, they meet their dream helpers who will remain with them throughout their lives (if they survive their first journey).*

In late August no rain has fallen for more than four months and herbs and the tops of purple needle-grass are brown and dry. A month ago, the women of Yihiwi, near Medea Creek, have gathered the needle-grass seed, beating the stalks with a deep basket and scooping in the falling seed with another, shallow one. Most of it will be stored to be eaten during the winter.

Shining Shell and her friends like to watch the women set fire to the dry plants. Soon flames are licking up the slope toward a stand containing elderberry, manzanita, bay laurel, and holly-leaf cherry, whose fruits and nuts will be ready for harvest in another month.

Fire creeps under the shrubs here and there, flaring up briefly when it reaches dead branches, dying down where the dried grasses give way to bare earth. There is little fuel to sustain the fire because this area burned three years ago.

The alarm-squawk of a scrub jay draws Shining Shell's attention to a red-tailed hawk rising into the brilliant blue sky above the chaparral, dangling a big gopher snake. Her mouth waters and she realizes, suddenly, that she is hungry.

Because of both deliberate and inadvertent burning, chaparral and coastal sage scrub were probably less extensive in Shining Shell's time than now and fuel mass was much lower. At the same time, thousands of years of fires encouraged the evolution of plants that put their energy into making nutritious flowers and seeds. Plants such as these, in turn, produced a happy, easy life for one of the densest populations of Indians north of Central Mexico.

Momoy. (jimson weed)

❧

On an October day, around A.D. 1200, a hunter from Siutcanga, another Fernandeño village, hears his dog whine softly and sees the animal's ears prick toward a grove of valley oaks along what we know as Caballero Creek. From the hunter's waist dangles a charm made of feathers of a sharp-shinned hawk, so I'll call him Sharp-one.

In silence, man and dog creep toward the trees and soon glimpse a small herd of mule deer. Summer drought has driven them to seek water in pools persisting in the creekbed.

Delighted, Sharp-one and his dog go back to the village to tell the tomyaar, *or head, of the wealthy families of Siutcanga. As they approach, three more dogs run out, barking and wagging their tails.*

Siutcanga is in a grove of coast live oaks, near the year-round warm spring still flowing in present-day Encino. Sharp-one's wife is playing in the spring with their baby. When the dog comes up to her, she jumps out of the water and runs to her husband, tying a soft deerskin apron around her waist. Holding the baby, smiling and laughing, she greets and embraces him.

His body responds to her warm, wet skin, but he pushes her away gently and tells her of his find. It would be bad luck to have sex with her from now

Rafael Solares making stone projectile points. (SWM)

until the hunt is over, perhaps because the odors of sexual activity would warn off the game.

Several dogs run out, as Sharp-one and his wife approach Siutcanga. About thirty circular houses stand in the cleared area, wisps of smoke rising from their high-domed roofs.

Lead-one, the tomyaar, gathers the hunters to plan the hunt. There are fifteen men in the group, including Sharp-one's brother, Smart, Smart's married son, and Sharp-one's own son, Valley-oak. After about an hour, the plan is set.

In the yovaar, or sacred enclosure, a high-ranking shaman draws an image of a spiritual being upon the ground in front of a figure of Chengiichngech made of deerskin and eagle feathers. Then Lead-one and the shamans march in front of the drawing, accompanied by those few hunters who had been initiated into some of the sacred rites. Only the initiated who had patrons among the elite can enter the sacred enclosure.

Lead-one springs very high off the ground, shouting loudly, with his bow and arrow poised as if to shoot in the air. Each of the others does the same thing, in turn. Finally, all of the hunters rub their bodies, especially inside their eyelids, with stinging nettles to remind themselves that they are strong and brave enough to be successful.

The hunters know the deer will be gathering to drink in the late evening and early morning. The next afternoon they set out with Valley-oak limping behind. A year ago he fell from a boulder and broke his leg and the bone healed crooked. He does his best to keep up with the others, who wait patiently for him, respecting and caring for him as they do for every member of their group.

Just before they leave the village, several of the lead hunters pick up deerskins with the stuffed head of the deer attached. Five approach downwind of the place where Sharp-one saw the deer and, as soon as they see their prey drinking, creep back to tell the others. Then Valley-oak and most of the hunters encircle the deer, staying far enough away not to be detected. Sharp-one, Smart, and two others, deer disguises held on with chin and *arm straps, sneak up on the deer from opposite sides of the creek, the rest of the hunters following.*

When they're within 200 feet of the deer, Smart and Sharp-one crouch and start moving with one hand on the ground, carrying bow and arrow in the other. Their bows, made of elderberry wood backed with deer sinew, are exceptionally powerful. Their arrows are tipped with stone, chipped by hand.

Keeping their heads down, they take a step or two and only occasionally look up to stare about, mimicking grazing deer. In a short time, they're less than 10 feet from their prey.

The first shots kill a big buck outright and injure two does. The injured does and the rest of the herd bound up the creekbed with the lead hunters shooting at them. Valley-oak and the others tighten the circle and wound several more. Trying to block the escape of one of the injured, Valley-oak falls and the terrified animal strikes his forehead with her hoof.

Several hunters follow the bloody trails of three does, finally running them down under the oaks. When it's all over, six deer are dead and two of the injured have escaped.

Blood pours from Valley-oak's slashed head. Sharp-one wraps his belt around Valley-oak's head and twists an arrow shaft in it to tighten it and stop the bleeding. One of the hunters starts back to Siutcanga to alert an herbalist to prepare a treatment for the injured man.

The hunters drink some of the deer blood but eat none of the kill, for to do so would bring misfortune, a belief that may have arisen to ensure the rest of the village would be fed. Instead, they use their stone knives to gut the carcasses and separate them into hind- and fore-quarters and start back to the village with the venison balanced on their shoulders.

Smart and Sharp-one drag Valley-oak between them. He is muttering incoherently when the herbalist meets them as they enter the village. Although con-scious, Valley-oak can't walk or stand.

The herbalist directs Sharp-one to lay his son in his own bed to rest. If he doesn't regain use of his legs soon, the herbalist will treat him using counter-irritation, for example, by having him swallow live red ants while the herbalist applies more ants and stinging nettles to his legs and feet.

Meanwhile, the other hunters stack the venison in a pile and begin to dance, mimicking the movements of the mule deer, chanting thanks to him for feeding them and investing them with his power, and smoking the ceremonial stone pipe of Indian tobacco.

The celebration goes on until morning. Then they butcher the kill and the taakwa *(divider of food) divides the meat among the families. Everyone sits around the fire, eating and joking, while the men retell the story of the hunt, embellishing it as they go.*

Later that day the women will dry the rest of the meat over the fire, saving the pelts and skins for skirts, robes and capes, the bones for needles, fishhooks, awls and wedges for splitting wood, the sinew for making bows, and the hooves for rattles.

❦

The tragic history of the Indians around the Santa Monica Mountains after contact with Europeans has been told many times. Alien European technology and diseases devastated them physically and culturally as they have done native people throughout the world.

In this chapter I have tried to convey some of what we know or can infer of California Indian culture and way of life. Much remains to be unearthed and analyzed, but, in the end, they must remain more of a puzzle to us than any other beings who have lived near or in the Santa Monica Mountains.

California mission Indians, 1890. (SBHS)

European Settlers
— The Changers

THE *SPANISH MISSIONS TURNED THE LANDS AROUND THEM INTO FARMS AND ORCHARDS* and wreaked havoc on the California Indians. Before 1824, however, Europeans had relatively little effect on the Santa Monica Mountains themselves and, up to 1900, European settlements, like almost all of the Indian villages, were at the base of the mountains, because dense chaparral, lack of water, and rugged terrain kept people from penetrating farther than Indians had already gone.

I have constructed the vignettes in this chapter around people and places appearing in the written record. Yet, history rarely treats people's interactions with their natural surroundings explicitly. Therefore, in what follows, I have imagined what these interchanges must have been and made up some individuals to flesh out the vignettes, so to speak.

In 1824, when Mexico declared itself free of Spain, mission lands came under control of the Mexican government and led to the establishment of ranchos. My first story deals with Rancho Guadalasca, whose extent and first owner (Doña Ysabel Maria Yorba) are in historical documentation. Jorge, Antonio, and Pedro are my creations.

❦

In the winter of 1840, Rancho Guadalasca stretches along the coast from the western end of Mugu Lagoon to what is now Los Alisos (The Sycamores) Canyon east of Nicholas Canyon. Inland, the rancho reaches nearly to El Camino Real.

Jorge and Antonio, the two California Indian ranch hands in my story, are looking for five head of cattle that have wandered away from Doña Ysabel's herd.

With them on horseback is Pedro Gonzales, the rancho's juez de campo (field overseer). A former soldier in the Mexican Army, he looks upon California Indians as untrustworthy children to be shaped and prodded into willing workers, and wants to make sure Jorge and Antonio don't wander off to join what's left of their kinfolk in the hills.

Weeks of heavy rains had stopped the week before and the men follow cattle tracks along a muddy game trail in chaparral on the north side of what we call "La Jolla Peak." They have been traveling about an hour when Pedro's horse suddenly shies and whinnies. The Indians stand still and sniff the breeze coming over the mountains.

"Oso (bear)," Jorge says, trembling.

"Si," Antonio says and turns around.

Adrenalin rushes in Pedro's veins. "Vengamos (Come on)!" he shouts, shaking his reata *(lariat) and pointing ahead. Like most Mexicans he is highly proficient with the* reata; *few Mexicans carry firearms.*

"No, señor," Jorge says, ducking below the level of the chaparral and running toward the ranch with Antonio behind him.

Scared witless, Pedro thinks, with a disdainful smile. He loves lassoing and strangling grizzlies. Besides, even though Doña Ysabel owns 500 head, she should not lose even five because two savages believe bears can be magical beings.

Pedro has followed the cattle tracks for a few hundred feet more when he stops short, face-to-face with not one, but six grizzly bears sociably feasting on what's left of two of the cattle. They had become mired in heavy mud where they'd tried to cross the raging creek through what we know as "Wood Canyon."

Unfortunately, the two bears closest to Pedro are females whose cubs his horse has nearly trod on. The sows rise on their hind legs, curl their bloody lips and growl, pawing the air.

The horse rears and Pedro blurts, "Sacre Madre de Dios (Holy Mother of God)!"

He hauls the horse around and rams his spurs into his sides.

The sows rush toward the horse, now galloping along the trail. Trying to follow the narrow path, the horse slips and falters.

The razor-sharp claws of a 300-pound grizzly rake the horse's haunches and he screams.

Pedro turns in the saddle and slashes at the bear with his machete, driving her back, while the others scramble toward him through the bushes.

Horse and rider pelt along the trail for several hundred feet until the bears give up the chase. It is only then that the horse slows and staggers, weakened

from loss of blood.

Thoroughly shaken, Pedro dismounts and leads the horse forward, which collapses before reaching the stable. Vowing to beat the savages within an inch of their lives for deserting him, he decides to get a group of vaqueros *together to clear out the bears around the ranch.*

Encino Warm Spring.

❧

The bear on the California flag is a subspecies of the grizzly bear, the same species as the European brown bear. Fearless and destructive, grizzlies often collect in groups of ten to twenty or more, especially where food is abundant.

Once, lots of grizzlies roamed the chaparral of the Santa Monicas. In fact, because the missions and ranchos introduced abundant food for the bears, in the form of cattle slaughtered for hides and tallow, up to about 1850, the bear population expanded.

Bears gathered around the ranchos, where Europeans killed or captured them, especially the cubs. When the gold rush brought armed Americans to California, within twenty years all of the grizzlies were gone, for a horseman with a rifle was more than a match for a bear.

Grizzlies harassed the smaller, black bear, which did not occur naturally in the coast ranges and counties south of San Francisco or in southern California. Since the demise of the grizzlies, black bears have spread (or been released) into several areas outside their natural range.

I set my next tale at Rancho Los Encinos, where the artesian spring still flows from under the mountains, and where Eugene Garnier, hospitable operator of the rancho, installed a famous restaurant on the bottom floor of the Garnier Building, now under repair after being badly damaged by the Northridge Earthquake.

Garnier Building before the Northridge Earthquake. (WS)

In June 1875, two (fictitious) doctors from Indiana, Jim Haggerty and Louis Edmunds, disembark from the stagecoach at the stop across the street from the Garnier building. They have written ahead to Garnier, asking him to have his Indian hands collect medicinal herbs for them to study. My botanist friend, David Hollombe, who specializes in the lives of early California botanists, says several, like John Milton Bigelow, had been trained as medical doctors and searched California for plants that had new medical applications.

Garnier welcomes Haggerty and Edmunds cordially, saying, as he does to every traveler (honest and presentable or not), "Mi casa es su casa" (my house is your house). The doctors lie down to rest in the adobe built earlier by Vincente de la Osa, who had bought the rancho from its original California Indian owners. The 2-foot-thick walls still hold the coolness of the night and air moves freely through the well-oriented building. Soon the travelers are asleep.

When they wake, an Indian girl brings a tray with goblets of wine, which tastes oddly familiar. They stroll out to the reservoir, beside which Eugene sits in the cool shade of coast live oaks.

On an impulse, Haggerty bends to feel the water. "It's as warm as bath water," he exclaims.

Of course, he would never undress to bathe in it—naked as a savage, as he would say. "I suppose it's cold in winter."

"No. Same temperature, year-round," Eugene says.

"How'd you like the wine?" he goes on. "It's made of elderberry flowers.

Flowers around the Will Rogers Ranch House.

ABOVE: Adamson house.

INSET: Peacock fountain at Adamson house.

The Will Rogers ranch house. (RH)

The Will Rogers stables.

"So that's why it tasted familiar," Edmunds says. *"My great-aunt makes it from a tree in her garden in Indianapolis. It's probably a different species from this one."*

"Elderflowers are excellent for treating fevers and flu," Eugene says. *(Elderberry flowers are one of nature's richest sources of vitamin C.)*

The men talk of traveling and sheep ranching (Eugene was formerly a French Basque sheepman) until the sun dips below the oaks. Then they dress for dinner.

The Chinese cook has prepared a feast of roast venison, rubbed with pulverized leaves of California bay, quail with stuffing flavored with leaves of black sage, roasted yucca stalks (tasting like baked apple), biscuits with manzanita jelly (tasting like apple jelly), *and California walnut pie.*

The doctors are familiar with walnuts and the use of bay and sage for flavoring, but roast yucca and manzanita jelly are new to them. The cook beams as they praise his creations and ingenuity.

Over brandy and cigars, Eugene gives Haggerty and Edmunds little bags of chia seeds, saying they are highly nutritious, neutralize alkaline water, draw out infections, and refresh and clean the eyes. The doctors are pleased to learn of these new uses of a plant in the sage family, which the Greeks knew for its medicinal properties.

They are too polite to mention they already know of applications of some other plants Eugene tells them about, such as bay leaves, blackberry, and California sagebrush. Plants related to these have been in the

European pharmacopoeia for thousands of years.

Unfamiliar native plants are a different story. They learn that dried leaves of big-berry manzanita make a soothing lotion for poison oak (an affliction unknown in Europe), miner's lettuce is an effective laxative, and yerba santa is called "holy herb" because of its many medicinal uses. Chewing its thick, fresh leaves quenches thirst, tea made from the leaves cures coughs, colds, and sore throat, and compresses of the leaves ease aches and pains and heal sores. When they are ready to go to bed, Haggerty and Edmunds are well fed in both body and mind.

❦

My next story takes place nearly sixty years later. Except for Juan and Raoul, all the people, horses, and places in it are in the historical record.

❦

One morning early in May 1931, Will Rogers looks over the top of his newspaper out the big picture window and sighs.

"Same old fog," says his wife, Betty, standing behind him.

"Can't even see the other side of the polo field. It was real thoughtful of Mr. Ziegfeld to give me this landscape window. I just wish it'd come with a guaranteed view."

[These days, even when it's not foggy, eucalyptus trees blot out the view but, from Inspiration Point, you can see what Will loved to look at—Santa Monica Bay and the back country, as well.]

"I must confess, I miss seeing the ocean and Catalina, but they'll be back one of these days."

Betty chuckles and pats his shoulder. "Patience."

"You know when I want something, I want it now."

Betty smiles, used to Will's spur-of-the-moment way of life. Perhaps his refusal to plan is what's given him room to be a world-famous trick roper, humorist, stage performer, lecturer, columnist, movie star, aviation enthusiast and, beknownst to only a small circle,

View from Inspiration Point.

philanthropist, all at once.

He pushes back his chair and stands. "Come on, Blake." (Blake is Betty's maiden name.) "Let's take a ride. I don't have to be at the studio till after lunch and I want to show you something."

They walk outside and Will stops on the grassy slope in front their white, frame house. It consists of two, two-story buildings joined by a patio. Will and Betty refer to their home as the Santa Monica ranch, though "It isn't really a ranch," Will says, "but we call it that. It sounds big and don't really do any harm."

He has some justification for making the claim. Lying on a mesa more than 100 feet above Sunset Boulevard his property was once part of the Rancho Boca de Santa Monica, which followed Santa Monica Canyon from the mountains to its mouth, or boca,

Jimmie, Will and Betty Rogers. (WRM)

at the ocean.

He gestures toward an infant vine tied to a column of the front veranda. "That's a bougainvillea," he says. "It'll have red flowers. I had Juan put it in yesterday."

"By the time you're through," Betty says, smiling, "we won't be able to see the house for the flowers." She has long since stopped being surprised that flowers delight a man with Cherokee blood.

Will grins and waves northeast of the house. "Like you can't see the hill, now." Masses of poppies, lupine, paintbrush, and tidytips glow from the hillside.

"Wildflowers are so beautiful," Betty says. "Even fog can't blot them out."

Will tilts his hat back and scratches his head. "I suppose they're not really wildflowers because Juan planted them. But, come on, I want to show you something else."

In the stables, Will saddles up Soapsuds, a speckled roan that's his favorite roping horse, while Betty mounts Chapel, once used as a stunt horse in silent movies. As Will leads the way up a well-trodden trail to the north, the fog seems to gather about them, isolating the sounds of the horses hooves. Now and then, the voice of a wrentit or rufous-sided towhee rises from the chaparral.

They climb about a hundred feet and break out of the fog, a white meringue below them nestled between the sunlit walls of Rustic Canyon.

"It's a relief to be out of that," Betty says.

Will motions to the ridge above the canyon, where a narrow path has been cut through the brush. "This is a new trail Lee put in for me." (Lee Adamson builds all the trails on the ranch.) "It'll make it easier to put out fires coming up the mountainside."

"Well, don't let the fire department catch you trying to do their job for them the way you did before."

"I'm not about to twiddle my thumbs when fire's coming at our home. Maybe these new trails will keep that from happening."

They ride Indian-file, as they call it, along the ridge. Here and there, white spears of chamise blossoms sparkle in the sunshine and soft clucks of quail warn of their approach. With a sudden whir of wings, a flock bursts above the chaparral and veers between the

horses, but neither flinches.

"I guess those birds aren't used to having people ride through their real estate," Will says.

About a mile farther, they turn to retrace their steps along the ridge and have gone several hundred feet when Soapsuds comes to a sudden stop and backs away from a whirring rattlesnake in the path.

"We're not the only ones that like the sun," Will says.

They pull their horses back a few more paces and wait. In less than a minute, the snake, buzzing all the while, slides off the path and into the brush.

A stranger would be surprised Will doesn't shoot the snake, unless he'd noticed Will's unarmed. Despite his early experiences hunting with cowboys, he never carries a gun and says he never killed anything in his life.

He pats Soapsuds and walks him forward. "Well, old feller. Either you're too old to get riled up or you're too smart." He grins. "Raoul calls him a sabino. I guess that means a savvy old coot."

When they get back to the ranch, Pedro, one of the stable hands, comes up to take care of the horses.

"Snakes are out," Betty says to him.

"I'm ready," Pedro says. He's as adept at lassoing a snake with a horsehair noose as Will is at calf roping.

Will enjoys roping best of all the things he does and even practices tricks after dinner on a stuffed calf wheeled into the living room. He gets a kick out of bragging that he is "death on dead calves."

❧

I constructed the next story, which takes place in the fall of 1933, with the help of Sylvia Rindge Adamson Neville, Frederick Rindge's granddaughter, who plays a role in the tale. All of the people, places, and events in it are true, though I have imagined details of dialogue and action.

❧

At that time, the Adamson family are spending every weekend in their beautiful beach house in

Malibu. Gorgeous tile decorates the home and surrounding structures inside and out, making this one of the jewels of Southern California. The site, on the southeast side of Malibu Lagoon, is part of the original Rancho Topanga-Malibu-Sequit.

One Friday afternoon in November the Adamsons set out as usual for the drive to Malibu from their home in Hancock Park in Los Angeles. They ride in a seven-passenger, Pierce-Arrow convertible that Mrs. Adamson had ordered especially made. The group consists of Merritt and Rhoda Adamson, husband and wife, Mrs. Frederick Rindge (Rhoda's mother), the Adamsons's children (Rhoda-May, Sylvia, and Merritt Junior) and Merritt Junior's nurse. He needs constant care for frequent, wrenching asthma attacks.

It's been raining, off and on, for the past few weeks and Mrs. Adamson drives slowly to avoid rocks and mud that have washed onto the Roosevelt Highway (now PCH) from the bluffs above. They've been on the road for about fifteen minutes when Sylvia says, "Mary Ann's spending the weekend at Louise Johnson's house." (The two girls are in Sylvia's grade at the Marlborough School for Girls in Los Angeles.)

"Without her parents to supervise her? I don't think that's proper for a twelve-year-old girl," Mrs. Rindge says.

Sylvia expected this.

"The Johnsons are very nice," Rhoda-May says.

Sylvia is surprised by this support from her older sister.

"I agree with your grandmother," Mrs. Adamson says. "Besides, the girls will probably skip their homework."

Rhoda-May and Sylvia subside and all three children, taught from an early age to respect their parents' wishes, are soon reading quietly in the back seat.

At Las Flores Canyon, a steam shovel is scooping debris out of the road and piling it in a mule cart. Nearby, another cart waits to be loaded.

"Glad to see they're keeping the road open on this end," Mr. Adamson says. "Maybe we won't have to go home by way of Camarillo this time."

Soon Mrs. Adamson circles the front garden and draws up to the patio. (It usually took about an hour to reach Malibu but this Friday the trip is a little longer.)

When the butler opens the front door, Mrs. Rindge again feels a glow of pride in the exquisite tile around it. Seven years earlier, she had established Malibu Potteries and hired Rufus Keeler to manage the plant and create the glazes that became famous for their color and clarity.

As though reading her mind, Mrs. Adamson says, "Such a shame you had to shut down Malibu Potteries, Binks." (Binks is the family's pet name for Mrs. Rindge.)

"This terrible Depression." Mrs. Rindge sighs. "It's ruined me."

"I've put your things in your room," the maid says, coming in from the downstairs guest room.

"I'm afraid you won't be able to inspect the ranch," the butler says to Mrs. Rindge. "All the roads are impassable."

"I expected that," Mrs. Rindge says. "I've brought lots of fancy work to do." Like many ladies of her generation, she spent long hours on embroidery and other needle work.

Mrs. Adamson goes into the living room and

Merritt Adamson. (SRAN)

Front door of Adamson house.

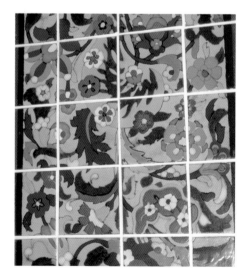

picks up a pair of binoculars. "There are even more western grebes here than last time, Smoke," she says to Mr. Adamson. (He had been known as "Smoke" ever since the Havasupai Indians had given him that name when he was a boy on his father's ranch in Arizona.)

She hands the binoculars to him and starts leafing through Dawson's Birds of California, lying open on a small table next to the window. "They're so handsome. I love having them here most of the winter." She learned to love nature from her father.

The family spend most of the next day outdoors, the adults enjoying Mrs. Adamson's gardens, especially the thriving coral tree she has set on the north side. Then they sit, sipping lemonade on the east patio beside the peacock fountain, decorated in deep tones of sparkling blue and splashing in the sunshine, surf rolling beyond. Nurse and the children spend their time on the beach.

In the late afternoon, heavy, dark gray clouds gather on the south eastern horizon and the wind freshens. "Looks like it's going to rain, again," Mr. Adamson says.

"If you'd call the children in from the beach, Smoke," Mrs. Adamson says to him. "I don't want Bunts getting cold." (They called Merritt Junior "Bunts" until he went away to military school.)

Mr. Adamson rises to go.

"Come upstairs to watch the storm come in, Binks," Mrs. Adamson says. The bedroom Rhoda-May and Sylvia share, as well as Merritt Junior's bedroom, open onto an uncovered porch that overlooks the ocean.

Rhoda Adamson. (SRAN)

By dinnertime, rain is drumming on the tile roof and continues, on and off, through Sunday morning. Rhoda-May and Sylvia do their homework, while Mrs. Adamson reads a mystery novel and Mr. Adamson finishes The Saturday Evening Post. Mrs. Rindge spends the morning on her needlework.

In the middle of the afternoon, Simski, who takes care of the Malibu Pier for the Adamsons, comes to the front door. Standing in the rain, hat in hand, he says, "The bridge's washed out so you can't go west, Mrs. Adamson. Road's completely closed at Las Flores and Big Rock, too."

"So there's no way to get back to Los Angeles!" Mrs. Adamson says. "We're cut off."

"You mean we can't go back to school?" Sylvia says over her shoulder.

"Swell!" Rhoda-May exclaims with a little hop.

Mrs. Adamson smiles. "I think you've had enough school for a while, anyway." She had had the privilege of studying with tutors until she was twelve.

So the Adamson family spent two weeks marooned in their beautiful Malibu home, with nothing to do but enjoy the natural world they loved.

❧

I've been able to tell only a few stories about the Europeans who first settled in and around the Santa Monicas. Some others were the Trippets and Stunts in Topanga, Herman Hethky in Cold Creek, and world-famous architects like Rudolph Schindler, who built homes clinging to the Hollywood Hills—but space does not permit. Though all these people loved the mountains, they all hastened the changes in mountain ecosystems that continue to this day.

Los Liones Trail.

CHAPTER 10

People and Their Hangers-On

AFTER THE DECEMBER HOLIDAYS, I BADLY NEED TO HIKE IN THE MOUNTAINS, not only to reduce my overstuffed body but to refresh my over-cosseted soul. I set off on the trail in Los Liones Canyon, climbing switchbacks up the mountain, passing under tall ceanothus chaparral, fifty years old or more—it's been at least that long since the last fire.

I stoop to investigate a rustle in the shrubbery beside the trail and see a common poorwill, one of our occasional visiting winter birds. Apparently unable to fly, it's threatening me with outspread wings and open beak. It must have been injured by a dog, for a coyote or bobcat would have eaten it well before daylight.

I'm lucky to be living so close to a mountain trail, with its wild creatures and wild plants, but sorry somebody's pet, on the trail illegally, has hurt this elegant bird. I scoop it up in my jacket to take it to the vet, for it won't survive otherwise.

One early morning in February, Bob Johnson (not his real name), who lives in Outpost Estates in the Hollywood Hills, sees a coyote trotting along Mulholland carrying something. Is that an animal hanging out of its mouth? he thinks.

God! It's a cat's head.

Heartbreak for one of his neighbors.

Damn coyotes ought to be wiped out.

He's driving too fast to see that the coyote is a female. She's pregnant and especially hungry during these days of relative scarcity. To feed her growing fetuses she eats whatever she can scrounge.

When Bob gets home from work that evening, his little girl meets him at the door in tears. "Mama says Missy's gone to heaven," she sobs. "And I'll never see my kitty again."

On the way to the kitchen, Mama whispers, "I found part of her tail near the fence. Something must have eaten her."

Now Bob is *really* angry at coyotes. At the meeting of the Outpost Homeowners' Association that weekend, he demands that all coyotes be trapped and removed from wild areas nearby.

"Without coyotes, we'd be overrun with rabbits

Injured common poorwill.

and rats," Jim Frances says. "Rabbits'll eat everything down to the ground. Including your garden, I may add."

"More coyotes will just move in, anyway," Lily Angstrom says, with some satisfaction. She's been feeding a female coyote, pleased she's been making friends with a wild animal. She hasn't realized that getting a coyote used to people all but guarantees the animal will come to grief, one way or another.

"Just keep your cat inside at night," Len Green says.

On that note, the meeting ends, though Bob is still furious.

It's early March, and Dan Mitchell (another fictional character), an aficionado of snakes and lizards, is looking in Topanga State Park for something to add to his menagerie. Rain has turned the trail into muddy slop and Garapito Creek is a rushing torrent, but that's why Dan has chosen this time for his search. Quite aware that collecting on park lands is illegal, he figures the risk of meeting a ranger is low.

By mid-day, sunshine is warming the creek bank. A thrill runs through Dan when he spots a snake, basking on the bank high above the water. Olive-brown, with stripes along the sides, it's a two-striped garter snake, still common along undisturbed streams like Garapito. He's never kept one and it will be a challenge.

For a long minute Dan scrutinizes the bank and strains to hear above the roar of the water tell-tale snapping of twigs or rustling of shrubbery. Nothing. He hopes.

Within 15 feet of his prey, he ducks behind some willows and approaches slowly. If he spooks it, it will slide into the creek, where it can remain for many hours.

Three feet away, Dan again looks and listens for signs of people. Still nothing.

He carefully maneuvers his snake stick, a pole with a flat-sided hook on the end, behind the snake. Then he smoothly advances the hook and, in one motion, slides it under the animal's body and lifts it off the ground. Without a surface for purchase, the garter snake hangs helpless.

He grasps it behind the head and it writhes, tries to bite him, and voids stinking musk from its anal gland. Unfazed, Dan holds it up and inspects it quickly, noting the relative shortness of the tail and narrowness of the tail base. It's probably a female, maybe with young, he hopes.

Bushes are thrashing. Someone is slipping and sliding along the trail.

Heart thumping, Dan drops his prize into an old pillowcase he uses for collecting and squats below the shrubs. Steps approach, go away. Dan straightens and sees a man's head down the trail.

When the coast is clear, Dan trots the other way toward his car, fantasizing about the emergence of a dozen or more little garter snakes next fall. (Like rattlesnakes, garter snakes bear their young alive.) Their

View of L.A. from Runyon Canyon.

fruitfulness helps ensure the snakes' survival, except where streams and lakes have been radically altered.

About a week later, a male flicker sits on a pole, lets loose a loud *kekekekekeke* and drums with his stout, woodpecker bill. The sounds resonate over the barnyard of White Oak Farm and are answered by a *kekekekekeke* as his mate of several years flies in from the oak woodland. The pair begin their courtship, bobbing their heads up and down and from side to side, calling *woika-woika-woika* to one another.

When they have renewed their bonds, they fly to an old valley oak nearby with soft, dead wood, just

Tachinid Fly. (DS)

American cockroach.

right for them to excavate their nest hole. The male fledged in this tree a few years earlier and ever since has chosen it as the place to raise their brood.

But as the birds climb up and down the trunk, a pair of starlings arrives, screeching. The male starling starts diving at the flickers. He staked out this tree in January and has already cleaned out the flickers' nest hole and put grasses and in it, courting the female starling meanwhile.

He pecks the female flicker on the back and head. The flicker, hanging on near the hole, tries to defend herself but the starling gives her a vicious jab. Meanwhile, by sheer *chutzpah* (for she is much small-

er than the male flicker), the female starling keeps the male flicker from diverting the attack on his mate.

Unable to avoid the starlings' jabs, the flickers fly into the branches of the oak and perch, watching for the starlings to leave.

Nearly an hour later, when the starlings take off to feed, the flickers enter the nest hole and start tossing out the grass. It doesn't take long for the starlings to come back and renew their attacks on the flickers. Just before dark the flickers leave the nest hole to watch from the branches of the oak.

The struggle continues the next day, each skirmish ending with the departure of the flickers, each

Bushtits. (MP)

beginning again when the flickers come back to reclaim their nest hole. But, after several days, they give up for good. Now the starlings have what they want and the flickers must excavate a new nest hole or face a barren spring.

Flickers have been in California for millennia; starlings are European immigrants, courtesy of a group of people who wanted every bird Shakespeare ever mentioned to live in America. In the case of starlings, they succeeded in spades. Since 1890, the first hundred birds, loosed in New York's Central Park, have exploded to many millions (billions?), reaching Southern California, in the 1940s.

As is so often true, many native birds cannot compete with the interlopers. In this case, though flickers can excavate new nest holes, birds like bluebirds that use abandoned cavities for nests are having a hard time surviving. We pride ourselves on having learned, from cases like this, to avoid introducing foreign species to an ecosystem. Or have we?

On a morning late in April, my friend, Marian, rests on a bench overlooking Runyon Canyon, while Jocko, her German shepherd, noses among surrounding bushes. She loves the view down the canyon, green and flowering this time of year, and Jocko has had a good workout, running up and down the

Flicker. (MP)

OPPOSITE: Hooded oriole on skirt of fan palm. (MP)

trail a full hour.

After a few minutes, Marian gets up and calls him, but he's found something he won't leave. As she nears, she sees him nosing what looks like a dead dog.

"Get away from there! Get away!" she says, running up.

Dragging Jocko away by the collar, she sees the body of a coyote. With Jocko whining and pulling against her hand, Marian inspects the corpse, a male, wondering what killed him, turning him over with her booted foot to look at the under side. No obvious wounds or bullet holes, no broken bones.

Could he have been poisoned? How sad!

Whoever did that used enough poison to kill a coyote. Or a dog. What a horrid thing to do.

Marian takes her pet home and calls the animal control people. When she tells the woman who answers what she's found, the woman says, "Another one! A poisoned coyote was found in Fryman Canyon about a week ago. We'll be right out."

Later, Marian finds out the coyote had eaten strychnine. Fortunately, Jocko didn't eat any of it, but. . .

In May, spring climaxes and Anna's hummingbirds, honeybees, and a pair of hooded orioles are battling for first place at my honeysuckle. With orange head and body and black wings and tail, hooded orioles are one of southern California's most striking birds. These are feeding three young in a nest in the skirt of a California fan palm a couple of blocks from me. Composed of dead fronds hanging below fresh ones, the skirt makes a wonderful home for orioles, whose numbers have increased since people started planting these palms as ornamentals.

Several place names—Palm Springs, Twentynine Palms, Thousand Palms—attest to the native fan palms that grow along streams and in oases in southern California but they are not native to the Santa Monicas.

On a late May evening, a young red fox, belly hugging the ground, sneaks through salt grass and pickleweed in the marsh on the western arm of Mugu Lagoon. Fog drifting in from the ocean deepens the twilight and settles in tiny droplets on his silky fur. He's after chicks he spotted earlier in the day.

The tide is out, and the parents, light-footed clapper rails (one of Mugu's rare birds), have led their brood of four, downy, black young to a mud-flat along a creek, to eat worms and crabs. The fox streaks down the bank to grab a chick, but the parents, instead of running off, turn and threaten him with their long bills. The two of them, each as big as a chicken, startle him, and he stops. A chorus of derisive, dry *kek-kek-kek-kek's* clatters over the marsh, revealing the source of the clapper rail's common name.

The ears of two nearby coyotes prick forward at the calls. They came into Mugu from the mountains last fall and have also been looking for dinner.

The fox has grabbed one of the adult rails by the neck when the coyotes come racing down the bank. The fox drops his prize and streaks off into the pickleweed, escaping certain death at the jaws of the coyotes. They bite the adults' necks and shake them dead, spraying feathers on the mud, then drop them to devour the hapless chicks before they can escape.

Loss of habitat has driven rails into pockets of marsh along the southern California coast. In these pockets the birds are easy prey to red foxes, originally imported to lowland California for sport hunting. Red foxes prefer open spaces like marsh and have, over the years, learned to live around people and eat chickens and other goodies. Wildlife biologists blame red foxes for wiping out ground-nesting birds, snakes, lizards, pocket mice, and other rodents at several spots along the coast that development has isolated from other wild areas.

In June, Lisa Bergen finds three big, bristly flies in her kitchen when she's in the middle of fixing dinner. She zaps them with insecticide and scolds her four-year-old daughter, MacKenzie, for leaving the door open.

You'd think, she fumes to herself, after paying a fortune for this new house, there wouldn't be enough filth around to breed flies. They must be coming in from those bushes below us. Lisa and her husband have just bought a home in Bel Air Crest above Sepulveda Pass.

A day later, MacKenzie has diarrhea and the woman at the day care calls Lisa away from the set she's preparing for a TV shoot. She takes MacKenzie to the pediatrician, who diagnoses a bacterial infection and gives the little girl a shot of penicillin.

"Could be salmonella," he tells Lisa.

"Isn't that carried in undercooked meat? I always cook everything thoroughly," Lisa says.

On the way home, she scolds MacKenzie again. "See what happened when you let those big flies in? They brought in germs that got in the food. Don't ever leave the door open like that."

She's being unfair to MacKenzie—the flies rode into the house in a bunch of roses from the garden. But Lisa is right to blame an insect for MacKenzie's illness, though she's fingered the wrong one.

The flies were clean tachinid flies that drink nectar while they search for cutworms to parasitize. The real culprits were American cockroaches, insects people introduce, inadvertently, wherever they settle. Lisa's roaches arrived hidden in bags of cat kibble. On their feet and abdomens, cockroaches carry bacteria they pick up from dead rodents and other debris they feed on and some of these bacteria, like salmonella, cause dysentery.

Many animal nuisances are part of our human baggage. Some are the cockroach, Argentine ant, ring-legged earwig, black rat, Norway rat, and numerous agricultural pests. By and large, these creatures bother people without disrupting native flora and fauna. Some, like the cockroaches, have native counterparts that don't hang around people.

In August, two months after the Bergens moved into their new home, they decide that Thai, MacKenzie's cat, has stopped trying to go back to where they lived before and let her outside—but only during the day. They hear coyotes howling in the canyon in the early morning.

Outdoors, Thai is in kitty heaven, a land full of birds and lizards that never saw a cat before. One afternoon she brings something into the kitchen and deposits it on the floor.

It starts waddling away, and MacKenzie crows, "Ooh, look it, Mommy. Thai's found a funny froggy."

Lisa runs in from the bathroom, afraid Thai may have brought a snake into the house. When she arrives, Thai has pounced on her treasure. She brings it back to the center of the kitchen and Lisa bends over a creature looking like the horned toads she's seen in pictures.

"Don't touch it," she snaps at MacKenzie. "It might bite."

Lisa quickly picks it up in a plastic bag, drops it in the toilet, and flushes it down.

Both Thai and MacKenzie are stunned. They wanted to play with it.

Thus ends another horned lizard, once one of the

Red fox. (MP)

German ivy in bloom.

Fox squirrel in Pacific Palisades.

commonest lizards in L.A. County. Collection by children, vulnerability to cats and dogs, its habit of basking where it can be run over, and fragmentation and destruction of habitat have all contributed to its decrease. In these ways, people and their hangers-on reduce the diversity of species in the land around them.

Thai is an expert hunter, like most domestic cats. In fact, similar to red foxes, domestic cats are top predators and can wipe out ground-nesting birds, reptiles, and rodents. They hunt by instinct, regardless of how well fed they are. Without coyotes to keep them in check, they would be as devastating to moun-

tain fauna as red foxes are to wetland animals.

There's always something going on in the cape honeysuckle outside my window, because it flowers all year. One September afternoon, for example, scattered tinkling sounds call my attention to a flock of birds busily jiggling it. There are too many inside the vine to be hummingbirds, though these visit the cape honeysuckle often, especially in summer and fall. When I catch sight of a plump, long-tailed gleaner, the size of an Anna's hummingbird, I know they're bushtits.

For a minute or two, the foliage shakes and wiggles, as they search leaves and stems for insects, twittering softly to one another. Then, to my surprise, one pulls a tubular, orange blossom to its bill with its foot and pecks into the base, without destroying the flower. Within a couple of seconds, it repeats the performance with another. It must be supplementing its usual diet of insects with the sweet nectar at the bottom of the bloom. Suddenly, the flock disappears and, suddenly, reappears in the guava beside the fence.

Except during the mating season, bushtits go around in groups of up to two dozen birds, all from a few family groups. A family—parents, offspring, aunts, cousins, grandparents, and so on—may contain as many as fifteen birds. Bushtits are common in chaparral, sage scrub, and suburban gardens around the mountains.

Guavas ripen early in October and fox squirrels, handsome, russet tree squirrels with bushy tails, use the utility wires running to our house as paths to our guava bush. People have brought fox squirrels, forest-dwelling animals in the East, into many urban environments. In southern California, they have not spread far from human habitation, however. They compete with us and with scrub jays and mockingbirds for fruits and berries in our gardens and rob nests, as well. Because of their agility, they are more devastating to nesting birds than are cats and dogs.

In mid-November, masses of little, yellow blossoms sparkle in emerald-green shade under oaks and walnuts near the mouth of Los Liones Canyon. These are the flowers of German ivy, which completely blanket the canyon walls and ground under the trees, ground that normally would be brown with leaf litter.

Leaf litter isn't the only part of the woodland that's missing. I see no ferns or sugarbush, no oak or walnut saplings, just green vines for hundreds of feet, heaving where they've overgrown and smothered plants that once flourished here.

With no saplings to replace the trees, in time the woodland will die. Above my head, vines are climbing on mature trees, threatening to do in even these, eventually to convert a richly productive woodland into a green monotony.

From South Africa, German ivy grows vigorously and is used in gardens as a container plant or for screening. People tossing cuttings into what they take to be a waste place, help German ivy escape into nearby wild areas. There, in the marine climate of the canyons where frost is rare, it takes over. I've seen no evidence of its being nibbled and many members of the family are poisonous.

Plants that behave the way German ivy does rank second in the damage they do to wild ecosystems. Of first rank, of course, is development, because it completely destroys ecosystems and, by fragmenting those that remain, disrupts their natural functioning.

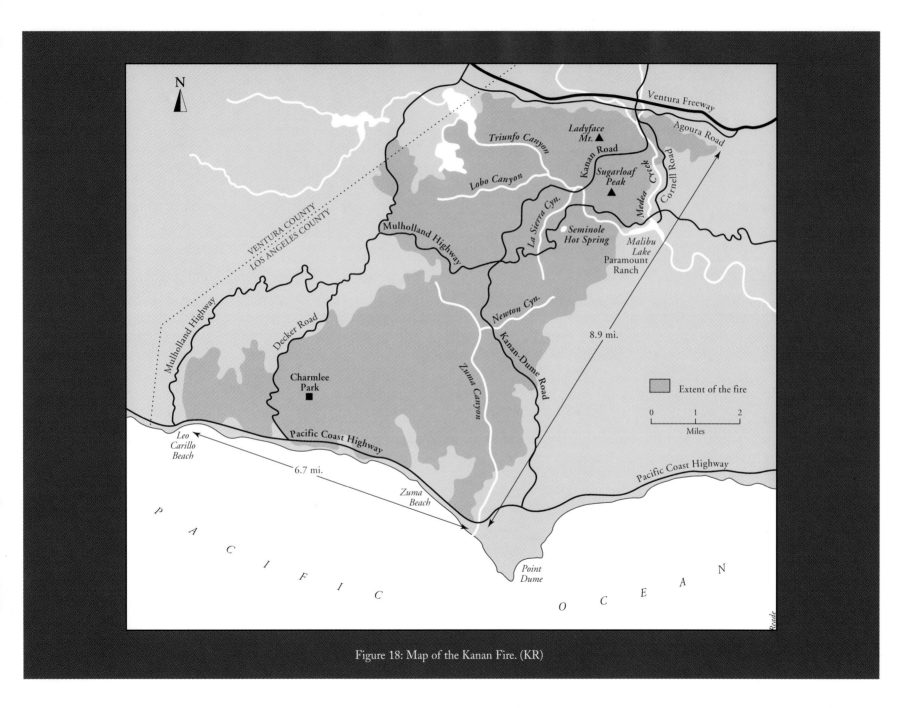

Figure 18: Map of the Kanan Fire. (KR)

CHAPTER *11*

Mountains Afire
— Death and Rebirth

AT 1 A.M., MONDAY, OCTOBER 23, 1978, SANTA ANA WINDS BEGIN BLOWING ACROSS the Santa Monica Mountains from the northeast and in half an hour the temperature at the L.A. Civic Center rises from 65 degrees F to 75 degrees F. Rain has not fallen since April and along Agoura Road the dry winds, gusting to 35 miles an hour, suck even more moisture from the grass. People who like to set fires know a strong, hot wind will make one hell of a burn.

In mid-morning, a teenager drives east along Agoura Road. He is furious; last night he had an argument with his girlfriend and he lay awake all night, getting madder and madder.

She'll be sorry, he thinks. He slows to toss several items out of his car. The sheriff will call them "incendiary devices," but they are simple—a lighted cigarette stuck in a matchbook. When the glowing end reaches the match heads, they burst into flame.

Some of the matchbooks go out, but three catch in the dry grasses beside the road. Heavy rains last spring brought lush growth that became what firemen call "flashy fuel" because it catches so easily.

The flames, pulled by the wind, sped faster by their own heat, climb the ridge south of Agoura Road. Figure 18 shows some of the landmarks in what will be called the "Kanan Fire" because it took off along Kanan Road. In 1994, Don Franklin, a retired L.A. County fireman who fought the Kanan Fire, retraced the route with me.

Almost at once, a woman in a commercial building along Cornell Road notices the blaze and phones the fire dispatcher. He sends a first alarm to Station 65 just up the road, which becomes the command post for battling the fire. The dispatcher calls other units and sets up a Strike Team, a group of five engine companies with two camp crews of firefighters and a bulldozer to fight the fire on the ground.

Within minutes after the fire started, fire engines, sirens blasting, are rushing toward it. By this time the flames have crossed Cornell Road behind the fire station and hurtled across Kanan Road.

The odor of smoke wakes a gray fox, dozing behind a boulder near the top of Sugarloaf Peak. He sniffs, jumps to the ground and trots over the ridge. A 60-mile-per-hour gust picks up an ember and hurls it aloft and he starts to run down the other side of Sugarloaf toward a dry streambed that crosses Paramount Ranch. Lucky for him, the land is still undeveloped and open.

Spot where Kanan fire started.

Sycamore over creek.

Oil-loaded chamise and laurel sumac explode in balls of flame, spewing burning twigs and embers into the sky and dropping them farther along the path of the winds. Dismayed firefighters watch embers sail above the east slope of Ladyface Mountain, to land in a draw they can't get to. In fifteen minutes a roaring hell engulfs the entire east side of Ladyface and turns the sky a fiery red. In mature chaparral, the accumulation of 400 tons of fuel per acre equals 1,400 gallons of gasoline. For a hundred acres, Don Franklin calculated, this translates to an energy content of one Hiroshima bomb.

As searing, thick smoke pours toward a pair of wrentits, they cling to the branches of a shrub, refusing to venture from the spot where they have spent their adult lives. Within seconds, they suffocate and drop to the ground. Although most birds and large mammals living in fire-prone areas have the sense to save themselves during a burn, smoke and heat kill many.

Racing south along Cornell Road, the fire approaches Paramount Ranch and homes around Malibu Lake. To the relief of the firefighters, Sugarloaf turns most of the fire into Triunfo Canyon,

Shrubs bent by Kanan fire, fifteen years later.

and cleared lands on the ranch slow its southward advance.

Firefighters' primary goal is to save lives and property. If a fire driven by a Santa Ana doesn't threaten lives or property, they don't try to stop it head-on. Rather, hoping to pinch it off, they fight it on the edges.

By now, the gray fox has reached Medea Creek and is running along the trunk of a huge sycamore leaning over the dry creekbed. Soon he perches well above anything that may burn. A hiss tells him a pair of great-horned owls shares his refuge.

A river of fire pours down Medea Canyon and devours the brush along the creek, and billows of smoke obscure the ground and choke the tree-sitters. But the swirling wind whips the smoke hither and thither and they find enough clean air to survive the fifteen minutes it takes the flames to pass.

In Triunfo Canyon, the roar of the fire scares a man hiking alone. He turns and starts running down Triunfo Creek, hopping from rock to rock, pausing to look back now and then. When flames top the ridge along Kanan Road, he takes a great leap, a rock turns under his foot when he lands, and he falls. His head

Burned land above Cold Creek.

Smoke over Malibu.

hits a boulder and he passes out.

With fire approaching in all directions, people in Seminole Hot Springs realize they must abandon their trailers. Some are crying and praying when a young man in a green car drives up and yells that he will lead them to safety. They form a ten-car caravan that starts crawling through smoke along Mulholland.

They hadn't known they could get out by taking Mulholland to Kanan to PCH ahead of the fire. Accurate information is hard to get during such a disaster.

The fire winds thunder at a hundred miles an hour, sucking up oxygen to replace what they burn, plunging down steep canyons, bending shrubs ahead of the flames, leaving bent skeletons behind. When winds are this fast, only the sea can stop the southwest rush of the blaze. With wry respect for their enemy, firefighters call the ocean "The Great Pacific Firebreak."

Smoke filters through the chinks of a dusky-footed woodrat's house in a bush in Lobo Canyon. She huddles in her nest, her life-long haven, and starts to pant in the rising heat. A fit of sneezing and coughing seizes her. In a few minutes she faints and, in a minute more, stops breathing. When a glowing ember ignites the nest, tenant lizards and bumblebees burn along with her.

On the ground outside, a brush rabbit scurries from a sheet of flames toward a clump of bushes. When she reaches what looked like a refuge, a blaze comes at her from the other side, and she turns to find herself surrounded. She dashes through the flames and her fur catches. Firefighters watch in horror as she torches a shrub twenty yards ahead of where they are working. Before she faints, she hears herself screaming.

When the smoke lifts from time-to-time, the people fleeing Seminole Hot Springs see woodrats

running about, some afire. Of the different kinds of rodents that live in chaparral, woodrats are the most vulnerable because they stay in their nests in time of danger. If they decide to leave, they often flee on roads where firefighters or panicked motorists run over them.

Beneath a burning shrub, several holes penetrate a pile of gravel and loose soil. A foot below the surface, a kangaroo rat waits for the fire to pass, choking and breathing as smokey air and fresh air alternately sweep through multiple passageways. Her distant relative, a pocket mouse, also survives in a nearby burrow. As few as 5 inches of soil is enough to protect burrowing creatures.

Little side-blotched lizards that hatched a few hours ago squirm on the dry ground, trying to find a hole to hide in. Soon the heat immobilizes them and a minute or two later, kills them.

Young creatures are always more vulnerable than adults. Most animals breed in the spring, however, and at this time of year their offspring are well on their way to maturity. Only the young of those few species reproducing several times a year are likely to be caught in the fires of late summer and autumn.

Thick smoke suffocates the man lying in the bed of Triunfo Creek and he dies before a river of flame reaches him on its way to Lobo Canyon. His jeans char and curl over his white skin.

In La Sierra Canyon the fire is so hot it burns the brush to the ground and leaves a denuded landscape like that above Cold Creek after the Old Topanga Fire in 1993.

The northeast wind, blowing at 60 miles an hour, roars up the canyon, sounding to firefighters like the "roar of ten thousand freight trains." At the intersection of Mulholland and Kanan the wind hurls embers ahead to ignite dry grasses in Charmlee Park more than 2 miles away.

An hour and a half after the fire starts, a pair of

Dusky-footed woodrat killed running from fire.

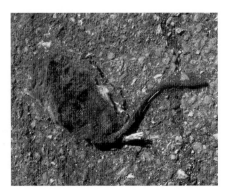

coyotes, red-tailed hawks wheeling and screaming above them, lead their half-grown pups to Los Alisos Creek in Decker Canyon. The coyote family drops into the arroyo along the creek, where a mule deer is standing. Neither deer nor coyotes heed one another. After the fire has passed, eyewitnesses will report it seemed to have imposed a truce among the animals.

The flames reach the banks of the arroyo and, as fire leaps among the oaks, scrub jays squawk and fly about and the coyotes dodge up and down the creekbed, shaking embers off their fur. When fire sweeps over the deer, she bounds up the bank.

Dull, gray billows of smoke hide the red-tails from view. Five ravens circle with them, waiting for the smoke to clear. They know from past fires they soon will feast on exposed animals dying on the ground or trying to escape.

Common raven. (MP)

Tens of thousands of butterflies, moths, bees, and all kinds of flying insects fall out of the smokey air or are borne aloft in the flames. Clinging to plants, beetles, caterpillars, grasshoppers, and spiders sizzle where they perch. Ladybugs, hibernating on the ground, suffocate together.

But hordes of western fire beetles fly in through the clouds of smoke and land on burning snags, smoldering leaf litter, and even firefighters, whom they nip with their strong mandibles. In their eagerness, some beetles fry themselves.

Most eat great quantities of dead and dying insects, mate near burning twigs and branches, and lay their eggs in cracks on freshly burned oak or toyon or, according to entomologist Chuck Bellamy, on whatever other plants have thick branches or trunks. Fire beetle larvae eat only the layer just under the bark and fire beetles are eager to beat their competitors to this food. Any fire (even one in an oil field) attracts the beetles. With heat sensors in a pit at the base of each middle leg, they can detect a blaze from as far away as 60 miles.

When the fire has passed the coyotes are only singed but the deer lies suffocated among embers on the bank. Ravens swoop down to her and scrub jays begin eating animals and insects on the charred ground, hopping up, now and then, when they step on an ember. They have several days of gorging ahead and weeks to come of plentiful food.

About two hours from the time it started, the fire, driven by winds of more than a hundred miles an hour, reaches the ocean. People and domestic and wild animals standing in the water watch shrubbery ignite homes along the beach.

By the time the firefighters control the blaze, it has swept over 25,000 acres, from Agoura to the ocean and from Zuma Beach to Leo Carillo Beach, and columns of gray smoke reach hundreds of feet above the mountains.

Not all of the land within the fire perimeter lies charred and smoldering. In some canyon bottoms,

Roasted ladybugs.

Unburned trees surrounded by burned land.

sycamores and oaks are only singed, and trees inside most oak groves are unscathed.

Unburned patches also remain on cooler north-facing slopes or where erratic winds blew the flames away before plants started to burn. Plants and animals in these patches will help feed the survivors and recolonize the burned land.

Many of the unburned areas, however, are where firefighters saved buildings and livestock. Rather than helping remaining wild animals and plants, these areas will impede their recovery. As more development scatters throughout the mountains, burned wildlands will have less ability to bounce back.

In two and a half hours, the Kanan Fire killed one person, destroyed 230 homes, some worth hundreds of thousands of dollars, and killed tens of thousands of mammals, including livestock and domestic pets as well as wild rabbits, rodents, and deer. No one will ever know how many birds, reptiles, and amphibians died, let alone invertebrates.

Except for its speed and ferocity, the Kanan Fire was typical. It was deliberately set during a Santa Ana wind in late October along an access route to the mountains. Accidents and human carelessness can also cause fires at such times. In fact, the day of the Kanan Fire, arcing wires set a fire in Mandeville Canyon that burned homes and other property worth more than eight million dollars.

On Tuesday, people and animals return to the remains of their homes and other possessions. Art Evans recalls that in some spots PCH was carpeted with the pelts of animals that survived the fire just long enough to be flattened as they tried to reach the sea.

Mountains that on Sunday were dark olive-green and Prussian blue, have become a gray-brown landscape. Shades of pale gray and umber blend with and subtly complement one another. Charcoal gray or burnt-sienna trunks and limbs reveal the forms of

Resprouting oak.

INSET: Roasted acorns.

Fire-gutted autos.

RIGHT:: Charred ceanothus.

New woodrat nest in tree hollow.

Spider webs cover a charred meadow. Their makers survived a few inches below the surface, which never got as hot as the surface under chaparral shrubs. For months, the spiders will have slim pickings, because few flies or other invertebrates have survived.

Sometimes, after she has finished the dinner dishes, a woman who lives with her husband in Decker Canyon looks out her kitchen window at the hillside once full of living things, and weeps. Every morning and evening for the past week, she's been putting out fresh alfalfa for several mule deer, seed for house finches, and corn on the ground. She never sees what eats the corn, but it disappears each night. It makes her feel better to feed the dispossessed.

She doesn't realize she's further disrupting their normal recovery by concentrating them around her home and encouraging dependence on people's handouts, which are usually less reliable than natural resources.

She shoos out a couple of homeless woodrats trying to nest in her kitchen drawers. They will have to start new houses elsewhere, and one begins building in the hollow of a sycamore.

She can feed only a few of the creatures near her home. The plants and invertebrates that support most animal life have disappeared. Hunger has driven bewildered deer into patches of unburned vegetation or out of the burn entirely, some into people's gardens, where the refugees must compete with deer already there.

The fire has consumed deep leaf litter, exposing a rich store of seeds for rodents to eat, but their populations soon plunge almost to vanishing, as the predators take their toll. Without shrub cover, brush-dwelling birds, such as thrashers, wrens, and wrentits, must either try to survive where there is nowhere to hide, or move out.

The Friday after the fire the teenager who started it all sees his girl with a group of friends at a mall

trees and shrubs like elegant sculptures above the ash and char. The dry air is acrid with the odor of burned vegetation and little swirls of ash rise around ones' footsteps. White ash shows where the fire found dense piles of dead brush and was especially hot.

On steep hillsides the burn has accelerated the fall of loose soil that gravity pulls down the slopes. Gusts of wind lift clouds of earth, like fog, above canyon walls. Where the fire was hottest, it blasted rocks to bits, further contributing to erosion.

in the San Fernando Valley.

"What about that house that burned in Trancas?" she's saying, acting like he isn't there.

"Worth 250,000 dollars!" says another. "That's a quarter million."

"Yeah," he says, pushing into the group. "Wonder who did it." His tone is knowing.

"Do you know who?"

The girls are noticing him now.

In a few minutes the attention goes to his head and when he takes his girl home he brags that he set the fire. Her parents overhear him.

He's disappointed when the California Youth Authority won't let reporters interview him because he's a juvenile. He won't be out from under the Youth Authority until 1988, when he's twenty-five.

In Decker Canyon, the woman listens to the morning weather report with apprehension and, every time dark clouds pass over her home, she says a prayer. The aftermath of a fire can be just as terrifying as the fire itself because, like most wildfires in southern California, this one came right before the rainy season. Heavy rain will sluice down the hillsides and turn the dry bed of Los Alisos Creek into a roaring river, washing people off the banks and sweeping cars downstream. If enough water falls to saturate the ground, the creek she has loved can become a river of mud, suffocating her and her husband in their bed.

Helicopters fly over the burned area, dropping rye-grass seed, which is cheap, sprouts quickly, and is supposed to hold the soil if the first rains are light. In fact, rye grass soaks up scarce water and nutrients and discourages native plants (whose seeds are already in the soil) from rooting during the first year after fire. Later, during the annual drought, rye grass dies off, leaving large, bare areas and sometimes allowing worse erosion. By the time I wrote this, most public agencies had realized that seeding after fire is at best a waste of money.

Burned oak.

In November, yellow-rumped warblers bypass the burned area, now empty of shrubs full of berries and insects, and robins and cedar waxwings look elsewhere for food. But mourning doves and meadowlarks arrive to forage for exposed insects and seeds, and woodpeckers from nearby woodlands are eating beetles and borers in the branches of charred shrubs.

Only two weeks after the fire, new spikes rise from the bases of singed yuccas and bright green leaves appear around burned chamise trunks. About half of all chaparral shrubs reoccupy burned areas by sending up sprouts from root crowns. Most burls, along with their supporting roots, survive just below the surface and don't need rain to sprout because they store water.

Tonight the coyotes are hunting in the burn

People on wildflower walk.

along Decker Canyon. In the light of the stars, one of the pups stops, ears pricked. He has heard something move and begins stalking soundlessly toward a chamise burl while the others watch. But a shadow floats out of the sky ahead of him. There is a tiny shriek and, with a few silent wingbeats, a great-horned owl lifts above the burl, a brush mouse in its talons. Hunger had driven the mouse to forage where the owl's keen eyes could easily spot it.

For the next year or two, until shrubs begin to cover the ground, many brush mice will die. Shrub bark, which makes up much of their diet, has been destroyed and they will be wary of venturing into the open, to find what food remains.

The next evening, a soft rain begins to fall. All that night, clouds of mist blow over charred earth and, by the time the shower has passed about a quarter of an inch has come down. The woman in Decker Canyon gives thanks.

Despite cold weather, the kiss of water is just enough to start plants growing without causing floods and mud slides. Several more showers follow and, by the end of November, more than 2 inches of rain have fallen.

During December, the temperature continues to drop and plants in unburned areas appear dormant. But on the burn bright green leaves burst from charred oak limbs and around stumps of shrubs that looked as though the fire had killed them. Quail fatten on acorns blanketing the ground under the oaks. The singeing has made them drop the nuts before they put out new growth.

On the east slope of Ladyface Mountain, a kangaroo rat nibbles new chamise leaves; nearby a cottontail has found fresh sprouts on a coffeeberry bush; and, in the sunshine on the south-facing slope of Newton Canyon, two mule deer that rode out the fire hiding beneath Big Zuma waterfall are browsing new scrub-oak leaves. By eating new growth, deer,

Parry's phacelia and poppies.

Eastwood manzanita.

rodents, and rabbits delay plant recovery but vegetation restores itself in many ways.

Tree poppy seedlings spring from the charred land in huge numbers. They come from seeds that won't sprout until fire stimulates them. Seeds whose germination is stimulated by fire are called "refractory."

By spring, more than 13 inches of rain have fallen and warmer days have started plants growing in earnest. Sprouts at least a foot tall rise among a clump of charred branches of holly-leaf cherry. Green shoots cover bare ground. Most chaparral and sage scrub plants produce abundant seeds early in their lives and these can survive extremely hot fires if they are well buried. Thus, though birds and animals have been eating exposed seeds, enough remain to create lush gardens of annuals, grasses, and shrub seedlings.

Almost overnight, sheets of light blue and royal purple, highlighted by brilliant splashes of golden orange, cover hillsides above PCH. Here, California poppies glow amid succulent lupine and Parry's phacelia, and, freed from the dense canopy of chaparral shrubs, lavender-tinted Catalina mariposa lilies, sparse in unburned chaparral, unfurl to hover like butterflies among the wildflowers. People drive up PCH to take pictures or stand in the fields of flowers, drinking in splendor and hoping to engrave the vision forever in memory.

Parry's phacelia is one of the most beautiful wildflowers in the Santa Monicas. Pure white spots at the petal bases set off royal-purple, velvety flowers, sometimes 2 inches in diameter. Dr. Parry, a botanist who visited the southwestern mountains during the latter half of the nineteenth century, could have no finer memorial.

Like the tree poppy, Parry's phacelia has refractory seeds, that is, seeds that need fire to sprout. These ensure that rather than trying to grow under a heavy shrub canopy where sunshine, water, and nutrients are in short supply, the plant will flourish in more favorable conditions.

Four ravens are taking turns at swooping on a female red-tailed hawk in Decker Canyon. She cannot fight back because she is sitting on two eggs in the new nest she and her mate built to replace the one the fire burned. They had used the old nest for five years.

When her mate approaches with a snake in his claws, the ravens turn on him, and one of them comes close to landing a vicious bite on his neck. It flies off when he drops the snake and turns upside down, claws extended. Another raven grabs the snake before it hits the ground, and the four thieves begin quarreling over their booty.

Several days later, the ravens gang up on the female red-tail while the male is out foraging and force her to leave the nest to defend herself. As soon as she flies up to get a better position, one of the ravens lands on the eggs and starts to eat them. By the time the fracas is over, all of the eggs are devoured.

In Charmlee Park, a ceanothus sapling, leaves intact, has plopped onto the ground during the night; a pocket gopher has eaten its roots. To the dismay of home gardeners and farmers, pocket gophers dote on roots, bulbs, and tender new growth. Many pocket gophers live in burned chaparral during the first three years after fire, when diverse herbs are abundant.

Seeds of herbs and shrubs have also drawn kangaroo rats from outside the burn, but there is enough food for them as well as for the kangaroo rats that survived the fire in their deep burrows. In June, new-born kangaroo rats further swell the population and the decrease in California mice and brush mice leaves so much food that deer mice breed prolifically.

Margaret Stassforth, a botanist studying chaparral recovery after fire, has seen dainty, white, urn-shaped flowers dangle below yard-high crown sprouts of Eastwood manzanita by the second spring. Like most manzanitas, it has rich, smooth, red-brown branches that rise from a basal burl.

On hillsides carpeted with Parry's phacelia the year before, different plants bloom: bush poppy, yerba santa, sticky monkeyflower, canyon sunflower. Deerweed, chaparral pea, and ceanothus flourish because their roots draw and retain nitrogen. By increasing soil fertility, these plants also improve it for other species. And here and there are stands of tall fireheart and scarlet larkspur, white and red, together.

Late in the second spring, a column of harvester ants carries bush-poppy seeds uphill to their nest on Zuma ridge. These have a fatty attachment the ants like to eat in the nest. They disappear into the nest hole, while others appear, from below, to discard seeds, now stripped of their attachment, over the edge. Eventually the seeds will roll downhill into another drainage and expand the bush-poppy seedbed.

One morning, what sounds like a melodious robin is singing along the Zuma Canyon trail. But robins prefer areas with moist turf and lots of earthworms, rather than chaparral. This is a black-headed grosbeak in full breeding plumage, a handsome bird with an orange breast and deep-black head and wings with flashy white markings.

Until now, grosbeaks haven't been around since the fire, because there have been no large seeds or fruits—no acorns, manzanita berries, or holly-leaf cherries. Now that young shoots have set fruit, grosbeaks have come back from wintering in southern Mexico and Baja California, and females are already on their eggs.

By 1981, grasses have replaced some other herbs in the burned area. By 1984, shrub sprouts as well as seedlings surviving the rigors of the first year or two begin to crowd herbs out. Shrub cover increases rapidly, and, by 1985 to 1987, the seventh to ninth

Bush poppy.

year after the fire, the land returns to chaparral and sage scrub, though cover is shorter and more open, with a different mix of species than in older ecosystems.

By fifteen years after the Kanan Fire, the chaparral and sage scrub have returned to their normal density and mix of plants and animals. Despite the human cause of the fire and its ferocity, thousands of years of burning have adapted these ecosystems to rapid, essentially complete return to their prefire status. Whether their resilience will continue as development infiltrates more and more land, remains to be seen.

Today, charred snags still punctuate the chaparral here and there and blackened shrubs still bend over Mulholland. In time, however, the Kanan Fire will disappear from all but the memories of people who lived through it, people like Don Franklin, who says, "I heard the fire roar through La Sierra Canyon like ten thousand freight trains and watched it pour like a river down Lobo Canyon."

Pair of nesting red-tail hawks. (HC)

INSET: Willow Creek Canyon.

Scarlet larkspur.

Black-headed grosbeak. (LS)

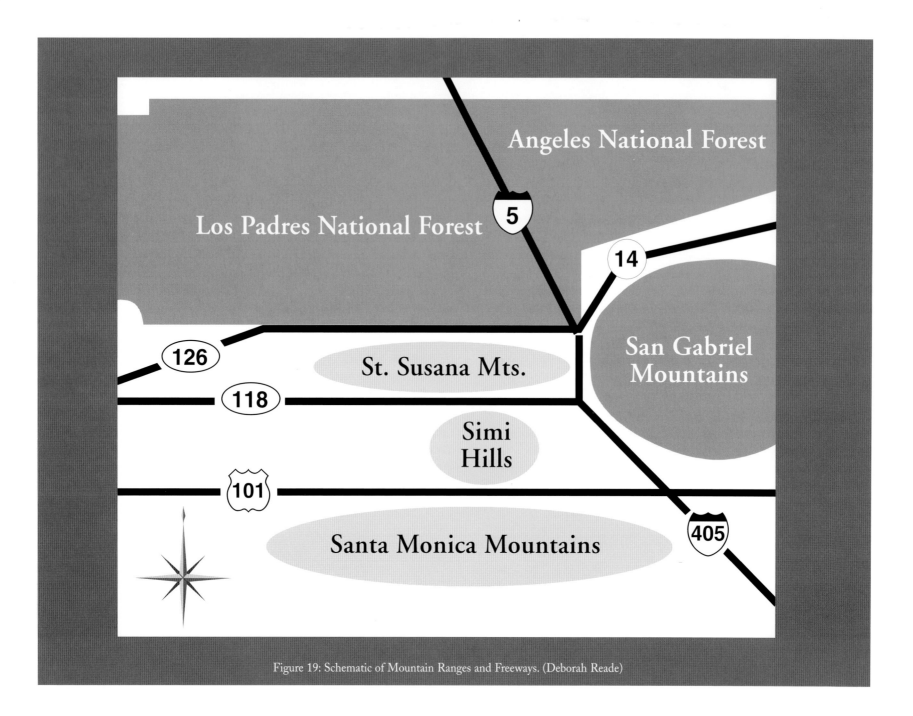

Figure 19: Schematic of Mountain Ranges and Freeways. (Deborah Reade)

CHAPTER *12*

Alternative Futures

ON A COLD JANUARY NIGHT IN *2015*, A YOUNG MOUNTAIN LION TROTS SOUTH *along Hummingbird Creek in the Santa Susana Mountains. Bordering the creek, remains of a kill and piles of leaves marked with the urine of another male warn him to keep going to avoid a confrontation that could wound or kill him.*

He crouches close to the stream bed, now and then lifting his muzzle to search for the other lion's scent. The breeze from the south is free of it.

At 3 a.m., traffic on the 118 Freeway is thin, and he lopes through brush beside it, looks over the gravelly shoulder, is buffeted by air pushed beside a roaring semi.

Going southeast, he reaches an equestrian tunnel and peers into it, but, in this version of the future, the reek of dogs drives him out.

Once again, he climbs up the bank beside the highway. Now, it is suddenly empty.

He bounds across it to the center divider, but endless headlights are coming at him from the other direction.

He flattens himself on the pavement.

Lights and noise terrify him, and he springs back toward the mountains he grew up in.

Blasting diesel horns, screaming brakes, swerving trucks, nothing can stop the killing.

In the 1990s, when Dan Preece leaves his office in Malibu Creek State Park late at night, he shivers, aware that a lion could be watching him out of the darkness. He knows mountain lions are deeply shy, and, if one were there, it would melt into rocks and bushes before he glimpsed it, the ghost of wildness.

Just the same, he thrills. A mountain lion is the only wild creature that could do away with him, if it chose. The state parks in the Santa Monicas are fortunate to have a caretaker such as Dan, supervisor of the Angeles District, who resonates to the wild land that surrounds him. In our world, people in positions of authority, like Dan, are key to the future.

Twenty-five years later, the young male lion, dead on the 118, may have been the last chance of the lioness living in Malibu Creek State Park for a successful mating. For several years her cubs, offspring of one of her own sons, have been stillborn. Next year, she will be too old to reproduce and soon she, herself, will fade away.

❦

In another version of the future, the young lion will cross under the 118 through a wide tunnel, free of the scent of dogs that have been fenced out of a wildlife reserve along the north side of the 118. He may come down Cheeseboro Canyon to a similar tunnel through which he will slip under the Ventura Freeway into a reserve opening into Malibu Creek State Park. Eventually, he will reach a young female, born two years before in a healthy population of lions.

Tim Thomas, a biologist who has spent much of his life in the mountains, has predicted that mountain lions, whose numbers he estimated to be down to seven or eight in 1989, will soon become extinct in the Santa Monicas. We don't know how such a loss will affect other animals and plants, but there will be effects, as the tales in this book have shown. Perhaps the population of bobcats will explode and wipe out some bird species.

The most obvious effect will be on people, for the wild heart of Los Angeles will become much tamer, taking another step toward becoming an urban park—a work of art, as Dan would say, rather than a work of nature.

Lions are a thrilling, heart-stopping symbol of wilderness, but other animals like badgers, golden eagles, gray foxes, bobcats, and clapper rails are also being crowded or driven out of their mountain and seashore homes. Are the mountains doomed to lose these wild creatures?

Tim and many other biologists believe losses could be stemmed, or even reversed, by linking natural areas in the Santa Monicas to each other and to the Los Padres National Forest and the San Gabriel Mountains, whose large, wild populations would replenish those in the Santa Monicas. Such links have been called "wildlife corridors," but many naturalists prefer the term "wildlife links" because it implies productiveness.

In 1990, Paul Edelman, an ecologist, laid out a plan for acquiring these links, which would include tunnels and overpasses crossing the freeways. Joe Edmiston, director of the Santa Monica Mountains Conservancy, employed Paul and adopted his plan.

Figure 19 shows how such a plan expands the scale and complexity of the Conservancy's responsibilities for the Santa Monica Mountains. In addition, the Mountains Recreation and Conservation Authority, an arrangement between the Conservancy and park districts to the north and west, has also expanded the involvement of the Conservancy.

Within the Santa Monicas, the 101 and 405 Freeways, Topanga Canyon Boulevard, Malibu Canyon Road, and surrounding development also impede wildlife movement. In 1989, Terry Ann Lieberstein, a biogeographer, created a scheme for linking Malibu Creek and Topanga State Parks. In her concluding pages, she cited dual, urgent needs:

1. for immediate action to acquire available, desirable lands, and
2. for additional research on wildlife links.

Since Terry and Paul constructed their plans, the Conservancy has largely focused on establishing links among the parks and with wild lands remaining to the north and east. Joe has made several deals by agreeing to permit more development than called for by area plans in exchange for the donation or sale of important parcels of open land to land conservation agencies. He is especially proud of having acquired a substantial piece between the Ventura Freeway and Cheeseboro Canyon after six years of negotiating with the landowners, political entities, and conservation agencies involved.

As of the mid-1990s, however, no links were completely in public ownership and connections between Malibu Creek, Topanga, and Griffith Parks were under assault or narrowing. In particular, freeways and highways remain major barriers to large mammals, reptiles, and a few species of nonmigratory birds.

As of this writing, lack of funds, politics, and development pressures are turning some public lands in the Santa Monica Mountains into biological islands largely isolated from each other and from adjacent natural areas. The extent to which populations of critical species are suffering depends on how freely species can move through private lands that are still undeveloped. Clearly, the longer land remains in private hands, the more likely it is to be fenced or otherwise changed in ways that hinder wildlife movement.

We don't know how much land the threatened species, particularly large mammals, need to live in the Santa Monicas or even the sizes and makeup of their current populations. Ongoing research on predators such as bobcats and coyotes in Cheeseboro Canyon will yield some answers for Cheeseboro and, by extension, for the Santa Monicas.

But we still won't know to what extent wildlife links will promote species dispersal, what should be the edge-to-interior ratios for various species and habitats, or answers to other questions basic to wildlife link design. We *do* know that, elsewhere, predators like ravens and domestic cats hunting along the edges of natural habitats have pushed remnant populations of birds and reptiles to the brink of extinction.

In the last few years, the National Park Service has concentrated on acquiring land in the still relatively undeveloped areas west of Malibu Creek, and, by this writing, has added 20,000 acres of the 40,000 originally planned for the National Recreation Area. Protecting highly productive habitats like riparian areas and oak woodlands, and rare habitats like native grasslands and salt marshes, makes good sense.

Land, or regulation of human activity, is also needed to buffer existing, high-quality habitat from human disturbance. For example, development should be set far enough back from park boundaries so that fuel-reduction need not be carried out *inside* the park. Similarly, contaminated water draining from the land, such as the farms east of Oxnard, causes what Steve Schwartz, in the Navy's Environmental Division at Point Mugu, sees as Mugu's most serious ecological problem and undoubtedly reduces biodiversity in the marshes and lagoon. Effluents into Calleguas Creek and other drainages would have to be cleaned up to solve this problem.

Lacking sizeable chunks of money for land acquisition, as at present, the objective of adding to or buffering existing reserves or establishing large, new ones competes with the objective of building wildlife links. For example, large blocks of land still to be acquired in the National Recreation Area include more expensive pieces between the ocean and Malibu Creek and Topanga State Parks and to the east of Malibu Canyon Road. Does this mean we must abandon to their fates existing isolated reserves, such as Topanga State Park, especially in view of the high cost of land surrounding them?

People who design wildlife refuges believe (and common sense suggests) that, in general, reserves that are large enough to support healthy populations of wild species are a far more effective way to preserve them than are links among reserves that are too small to do the job on their own. Given the high cost of land in the Santa Monicas, however, effective links among the parks and to large, natural ecosystems to the north and east could make better economic sense.

The National Park Service, California State Parks, and the Santa Monica Mountains Conservancy operate within and across numerous political jurisdictions—the city of Los Angeles, Los Angeles County, Ventura County, and several incorporated cities like Malibu and Calabasas. Overlying these political divisions, the California Coastal Commission regulates construction on the seaward side of the range.

The complexity of these overlapping arrangements has worse consequences than loss of communication between key decision-makers and confusion of the general public. Environmental concerns are interrelated, but local governments, and state and federal agencies, must protect their own jurisdictions. The six-year controversy surrounding the eventual acquisition of the land between Cheeseboro Canyon and the Ventura Freeway dramatically illustrates the results of having different jurisdictions involved with land-use decisions.

Arthur Eck, the new superintendent of the Santa Monica Mountains National Recreation Area, has committed the National Park Service, California State Parks, and the Santa Monica Mountains Conservancy to improved cooperation and exchange of information. Without funds for more than the day-to-day operation of the National Recreation Area, however, the federal role must be essentially an informative and advisory one at present.

In general, the various jurisdictions agree about the purpose of land acquisition and development in the mountains. Unfortunately, however, selfish objectives or overemphasis on points of *dis*agreement often discourage county, state or federal policy-makers from investing taxpayers' money in land for the Santa Monicas. To obtain broad political support for land conservation, the leaders involved must be willing to forego parochial interests and adopt a more united approach.

What are the possibilities for the Santa Monicas over the longer run? Two changes are certain: continued growth in the human population living around the mountains and shifts in population composition. Although the population of L.A. County has remained about the same over several years, the National Park Service predicts that sometime after the turn of the century, nearly 7 percent of the population of the United States will live in southern California.

The belief in many cultures that people's wants always take precedence poses the danger that the Santa Monicas might become a series of large picnic areas, amusement parks, soccer fields, rock-climbing areas, and the like.

This was not the intent of Congress when the National Recreation Area was established, to:

> preserve and enhance its scenic, natural, and historical setting . . . while providing for the recreational and educational needs of the visiting public.

Easier said than done. Often preservation and enhancement of the natural setting conflict even with people's love of nature. For example, most spectacular displays of spring flowers are inaccessible to people physically unable to walk more than a few paces, but few flowers would remain if roads and other facilities were built to accommodate everyone.

Given half a chance, nature's beauty and fascination make its own converts. Youngsters are particularly susceptible, but adults, too, can fall in love with the mountains during a single hike.

Over the long run, opportunities for young people to enjoy nature are essential to the survival of natural ecosystems in the mountains. An annual field trip to the mountains for every school child would be an important part of such a program. Several agencies and docent organizations succeed in exposing nearly half of the L.A. school population to the mountains annually. This is a surprisingly large fraction, considering that volunteers staff most such programs.

But field trips alone don't make up for the kind of daily experience of the natural world that I grew up with and from which I learned to love nature. For this, a child doesn't need access to wilderness, however. Wild creatures in natural parks and undeveloped land within walking distance of home can stimulate a child's imagination and excitement with the natural world.

Los Angeles is poverty-stricken in parkland, which may partly explain why the largest proportion of votes for park bonds comes from inner city neighborhoods. Many small natural parks throughout the city would both serve and educate the public and, at the same time, relieve some of the pressure on the Santa Monicas.

In the past, newcomers have needed only one generation to shift their attitudes toward those of the dominant culture. Most southern Californians enjoy the natural world, but relatively few care for it for its own sake. Can the numbers of those who appreciate it in this way be expanded soon enough to sweep the newcomers with them?

Even if they do, can the Santa Monicas survive the human onslaught? In keeping with his penchant for big-thinking, Joe Edmiston sees areas like the Angeles and Cleveland National Forests as essential safety valves for drawing urban pressures off the Santa Monicas. In this sense, more distant natural areas are also part of the Santa Monica Mountains ecosystem, and the health of the wild heart of Los Angeles depends on them as well as what goes on within and immediately surrounding the mountains. Thus, the prognosis for the Santa Monicas depends on southern Californians' depth of appreciation for the natural world as a whole.

References

Chapter 1

Brenzel, Kathleen N., ed. 1995. *Sunset Western Garden Book.* Sunset Publishing Corporation, Menlo Park, CA.

Brilliant, Ashleigh E. 1964. *Social Effects of the Automobile in Southern California during the Nineteen-Twenties.* Ph.D. dissertation in History, University of California, Berkeley.

California Department of Parks and Recreation. 1989. "Point Mugu State Park," "Malibu Creek State Park" and "Topanga State Park." One-page handouts available through: Department of Parks and Recreation, P.O. Box 94286, Sacramento, CA 94296-0001.

Crespi, Padre Juan. 1769-1770. *Unpublished Diary.*

Gebhard, David, and Robert Winter. 1994. *Los Angeles. An Architectural Guide.* Gibbs Smith, P.O. Box 667, Layton, UT 84041.

Gustafson, Sarah. March 1994. *Santa Cruz Island Reserve.* The Nature Conservancy of California, 213 Stearns Wharf, Santa Barbara, CA 93101.

Jorgen, Randolph. 1995. *Mountains to Ocean. A Guide to the Santa Monica Mountains National Recreation Area.* Southwest Parks and Monuments Association, Tucson, AZ.

King, Chester. July 18, 1994. *Prehistoric Native American Cultural Sites in the Santa Monica Mountains.* Topanga Anthropological Consultants, P.O. Box 826, Topanga, CA 90290.

Los Angeles Department of Parks and Recreation. Undated. "Griffith Park." Descriptive pages available from: Park Ranger Headquarters, 4730 Crystal Springs Drive, Los Angeles, CA 90027.

Marinacci, Barbara, and Rudy Marinacci. 1980. *California's Place Names.* Tioga Publishing Co., Palo Alto, CA.

McManus, Reed. November-December 1992. Place Setting. *Sierra* 77(6).

Santa Monica Mountains National Recreation Area. January 1987. *Land Protection Plan for Santa Monica Mountains National Recreation Area and Addendum.* National Park Service.

Rindge, Frederick H. 1898. *Happy Days in Southern California.* Available from the Malibu Historical Society.

York, Louise Armstrong, ed. 1992. *The Topanga Story.* The Topanga Historical Society.

Chapter 2

Atwater, Tanya. 1970. Implications of Plate Tectonics for the Cenozoic Tectonic Evolution of Western North America. *Geological Society of America Bulletin* 81, pp. 3513-3536.

Blackburn, Thomas C. 1975. *December's Child. A Book of Chumash Oral Narratives.* University of California Press, Berkeley, Los Angeles, London.

Dickenson, William R. 1981. Plate Tectonics and the Continental Margin of California. In W.G. Ernst, ed. *The Geotectonic Development of California.* Prentice-Hall, Englewood Cliffs, NJ.

Gustafson, Sarah. March 1994. *Santa Cruz Island Reserve.* The Nature Conservancy of California, 213 Stearns Wharf, Santa Barbara, CA 903101.

Hogue, Charles L. 1993. *Insects of the Los Angeles Basin.* Natural History Museum of Los Angeles County.

Hotz, Robert Lee. January 13 and December 8, 1995. *Los Angeles Times.*

Keeley, Jon E., and Sterling C. Keeley. 1987. Chaparral. In Michael G. Barbour and William Dwight Billings, eds. *North American Terrestrial Vegetation,* pp. 165-207. Cambridge University Press, Cambridge, New York, New Rochelle, Melbourne, Sydney.

Lebow, Ruth. 1993. Introduction to the Geology. *The Natural and Cultural History of the Santa Monica Mountains.* UCLA Extension.

Levy, Lou, ed. 1980. *Day Walks in the Santa Monica Mountains.* Santa Monica Mountains Task Force of the Los Angeles Chapter of the Sierra Club.

McAuley, Milt. 1991. *Hiking Trails of the Santa Monica Mountains.* Canyon Publishing Co., 8561 Eatough Avenue, Canoga Park, CA 91304.

McPhee, John. 1993. *Assembling California.* Farrar, Straus and Giroux, New York.

National Park Service. 1992. "Santa Monica Mountains. Cheeseboro Canyon Site."

Onuf, Christopher P. 1987. *The Ecology of Mugu Lagoon, California: An Estuarine Profile.* US Fish and Wildlife Service. Biological Report 85(7.15).

Raven, Peter H., Henry J. Thompson, and Barry A. Prigge. 1986. *Flora of the Santa Monica Mountains, California.* Southern California Botanists, Special Publication No. 2.

Whitney, Stephen. 1979. *The Sierra Nevada.* Sierra Club Books. San Francisco.

York, Louise Armstrong, ed. 1992. *The Topanga Story.* The Topanga Historical Society.

Chapter 3

Barbour, Michael G., and Jack Major, eds. 1988. *Terrestrial Vegetation of California.* California Native Plant Society. Special Publication Number 9.

Barbour, Roger W., and Wayne H. Davis. 1969. *Bats of America.* University Press of Kentucky.

Barth, Friedrich G. 1991. *Insects and Flowers. The Biology of a Partnership.* Princeton University Press, Princeton, NJ.

Bright, William. 1993. *A Coyote Reader.* University of California Press. Berkeley, Los Angeles, Oxford.

De Lisle, Harold, Gilbert Cantu, Jerrold Feldner, Paul O'Connor, Max Peterson, and Philip Brown. 1986. *The Distribution and Present Status of the Herpetofauna of the Santa Monica Mountains.* Southwestern Herpetologists Society.

Grant, Karen A., and Verne Grant. 1968. *Hummingbirds and Their Flowers.* Columbia University Press, New York and London.

Gruson, Edward S. 1972. *Words for Birds.* Quadrangle Books, New York.

Hogue, Charles L. 1993. *Insects of the Los Angeles*

Basin. Natural History Museum of Los Angeles County.

Hovore, Frank T. 1979. Rain Beetles. Small Things Wet and Wonderful. *Terra* 17(4):10-14.

Ingles, Lloyd G. 1965. *Mammals of the Pacific States.* Stanford University Press, Stanford, CA.

Jameson, E.W. Jr., and Hans J. Peeters. 1988. *California Mammals.* University of California Press, Berkeley, Los Angeles, London.

Keeley, Jon E. 1991. Seed Germination and Life History Syndromes in the California Chaparral. *The Botanical Review,* April-June, pp. 81-116. The New York Botanical Garden.

Keeley, Jon E., and Sterling C. Keeley. 1987. Chaparral. In Michael G. Barbour and William Dwight Billings, eds., *North American Terrestrial Vegetation,* pp. 165-207. Cambridge University Press, Cambridge, New York, New Rochelle, Melbourne, Sydney.

Klauber, Laurence Monroe. 1982. *Rattlesnakes: Their Habits, Life Histories, and Influence on Mankind.* University of California Press, Berkeley, CA. (Abridged by Karen Harvey McClung.)

McFarland, Noel. 1965. The Moths (Macroheterocera) of a Chaparral Plant Association in the Santa Monica Mountains of Southern California. *Journal of Research on Lepidoptera* 4(1):43-74.

Quinn, Ronald D. 1990. *Habitat Preferences and Distribution of Mammals in California Chaparral.* Research Paper PSW-202. Pacific Southwest Research Station, Berkeley, CA.

Raven, Peter H., Henry J. Thompson, and Barry A. Prigge. 1986. *Flora of the Santa Monica Mountains, California.* Southern California Botanists, Special Publication No. 2.

Roeder, Kenneth D. April 1968. Moths and Ultrasound. In Garret Hardin, ed., *39 Steps to Biology.* Readings from the *Scientific American.* W. H. Freeman and Company, 660 Market Street, San Francisco, CA 94104.

Schoenherr, Allan A. 1992. *A Natural History of California.* California Natural History Guide 56. University of California Press. Berkeley, Los Angeles, Oxford.

Terres, John K. 1980. *The Audubon Society Encyclopedia of North American Birds.* Alfred A. Knopf, New York.

Tyrrell, Esther Quesada, and Robert A. Tyrrell. 1985. *Hummingbirds--Their Life and Behavior.* Crown Publishing Co., New York.

Wallace, Robert A. 1980. *How They Do It.* William Morrow and Company, NY.

Weathers, Wesley W. 1983. *Birds of Southern California's Deep Canyon.* University of California Press, Berkeley, Los Angeles, London.

Wenner, Adrian M. July 1, 1992. "Feral Honey Bee Removal on Santa Cruz Island." U.C. Santa Barbara.

Winston, Mark L. 1987. *The Biology of the Honeybee.* Harvard University Press, Cambridge, MA, London.

Chapter 4

Barbour, Michael G., and Jack Major, eds. 1988. *Terrestrial Vegetation of California.* California Native Plant Society. Special Publication Number 9.

Blackburn, Thomas C., and Kat Anderson. 1993. *Before the Wilderness.* Ballena Press, Menlo Park.

Clarke, Charlotte Bringle. 1977. *Edible and Useful Plants of California.* University of California Press, Berkeley, Los Angeles, Oxford.

De Lisle, Harold, Gilbert Cantu, Jerrold Feldner, Paul O'Connor, Max Peterson, and Philip Brown. 1986. *The Distribution and Present Status of the Herpetofauna of the Santa Monica Mountains.* Southwestern Herpetologists Society.

Disney, Walt. Sequence showing fight between tarantula and tarantula hawk in the nature film, "The Living Desert."

Farrand, John Jr., ed. 1983. *The Audubon Society Master Guide to Birding*. Alfred A. Knopf, New York.

Garrett, Kimball. 1992-1995. Interviews. Curator of Ornithology at the Los Angeles County Museum of Natural History.

Garth, John S., and J. W. Tilden. 1986. *California Butterflies*. Natural History Guides 51. University of California Press, Berkeley, Los Angeles, Oxford.

Hogue, Charles L. 1993. *Insects of the Los Angeles Basin*. Natural History Museum of Los Angeles County.

Jameson, E. W. Jr., and Hans J. Peeters. 1988. *California Mammals*. University of California Press, Berkeley, Los Angeles, London.

Milne, Lorus J., and Margery Milne. 1980. *The Audubon Society Field Guide to North American Insects and Spiders*. Alfred A. Knopf, New York.

Pavlik, Bruce M., et al. 1991. *Oaks of California*. Cachuma Press.

Powell, Jerry A., and Charles L. Hogue. 1979. *California Insects*. Natural History Guides 44. University of California Press, Berkeley, Los Angeles, Oxford.

San Francisco Bay National Wildlife Refuge. 1992. *Salt Marsh Manual*.

Schoenherr, Allan A. 1992. *A Natural History of California*. California Natural History Guide 56. University of California Press, Berkeley, Los Angeles, Oxford.

Terres, John K. 1980. *The Audubon Society Encyclopedia of North American Birds*. Alfred A. Knopf, New York.

Thomas, Tim. November 21, 1991. Proposed Candidate Endangered and Threatened Wildlife, Santa Monica Mountains National Recreation Area. *Federal Register* 56(225).

Weathers, Wesley W. 1983. *Birds of Southern California's Deep Canyon*. University of California Press, Berkeley, Los Angeles, London.

Whitaker, John O. Jr. 1980. *The Audubon Society Field Guide to North American Mammals*. Alfred A. Knopf, New York.

Wilson, E. O. 1971. *Insect Societies*. Harvard University Press, Cambridge, MA.

Chapter 5

Blackburn, Thomas C., and Kat Anderson. 1993. *Before the Wilderness*. Ballena Press, Menlo Park.

Chartkoff, Joseph L., and Kerry Kona Chartkoff. 1984. *The Archaeology of California*. Stanford University Press, Stanford, CA.

Emmel, Thomas C., and John F. Emmel. 1973. *The Butterflies of Southern California*. Natural History Museum of Los Angeles County.

Foelix, Rainer F. 1982. *Biology of Spiders*. Harvard University Press, Cambridge, MA, and London.

Hogue, Charles L. 1993. *Insects of the Los Angeles Basin*. Natural History Museum of Los Angeles County.

Jameson, E. W. Jr., and Hans J. Peeters. 1988. *California Mammals*. University of California Press, Berkeley, Los Angeles, London.

Mattoni, Rudi. 1990. *Butterflies of Greater Los Angeles*. Center for Conservation of Biodiversity/Lepidoptera Research Foundation, Beverly Hills, CA.

Milne, Lorus J., and Margery Milne. 1980. *The Audubon Society Field Guide to North American Insects and Spiders*. Alfred A. Knopf, New York.

Pavlik, Bruce M., et al. 1991. *Oaks of California*. Cachuma Press.

Powell, Jerry A., and Charles L. Hogue. 1979. *California Insects*. Natural History Guides 44.

University of California Press, Berkeley, Los Angeles, Oxford.

Quinn, Ronald D. 1990. *Habitat Preferences and Distribution of Mammals in California Chaparral.* Research Papaer PSW-202. Pacific Southwest Research Station, Berkeley, CA.

Raven, Peter H., Henry J. Thompson, and Barry A. Prigge. 1986. *Flora of the Santa Monica Mountains, California.* Southern California Botanists, Special Publication No. 2.

Roach, Arthur J. 1992. Topanga Fungi. In Louise Armstrong Young, ed. *The Topanga Story.* The Topanga Historical Society.

Stebbins, Robert C. 1985. *Western Reptiles and Amphibians.* Peterson Field Guide Series. Houghton Mifflin Company, Boston.

Terres, John K. 1980. *The Audubon Society Encyclopedia of North American Birds.* Alfred A. Knopf, New York.

Whitaker, John O. Jr. 1980. *The Audubon Society Field Guide to North American Mammals.* Alfred A. Knopf, New York.

Chapter 6

Clarke, Herbert. 1989. *An Introduction to Southern California Birds.* Mountain Press, Missoula.

De Lisle, Harold, Gilbert Cantu, Jerrold Feldner, Paul O'Connor, Max Peterson, and Philip Brown. 1986. *The Distribution and Present Status of the Herpetofauna of the Santa Monica Mountains.* Southwestern Herpetologists Society.

Hogue, Charles L. 1993. *Insects of the Los Angeles Basin.* Natural History Museum of Los Angeles County.

Jameson, E. W. Jr., and Hans J. Peeters. 1988. *California Mammals.* University of California Press, Berkeley, Los Angeles, London.

Kats, Lee B., Sean A. Elliott, and John Currens.

1992. Intraspecific Oophagy in Stream-Breeding California Newts *(Taricha torosa). Herpetological Review* 23(1):7-8.

McAuley, Milt. 1996. *Wildflowers of the Santa Monica Mountains.* 2nd ed. Canyon Publishing Co., Canoga Park, CA 91304.

Milne, Lorus J., and Margery Milne. 1980. The *Audubon Society Field Guide to North American Insects and Spiders.* Alfred A. Knopf, New York.

Orloff, Susan. 1988. Present Distribution of Ringtails in California. *California Fish and Game* 74(4):196-202.

Powell, Jerry A., and Charles L. Hogue. 1979. *California Insects.* Natural History Guides 44. University of California Press, Berkeley, Los Angeles, Oxford.

Stebbins, Robert C. 1985. *Western Reptiles and Amphibians.* Peterson Field Guide Series. Houghton Mifflin Company, Boston.

Whitaker, John O. Jr. 1980. *The Audubon Society Field Guide to North American Mammals.* Alfred A. Knopf, New York.

Chapter 7

Barth, Friedrich G. 1991. *Insects and Flowers. The Biology of a Partnership.* Princeton University Press, Princeton, NJ.

Clarke, Herbert. 1989. *An Introduction to Southern California Birds.* Mountain Press, Missoula.

Fitch, John E., and Robert J. Lavenberg. 1971. *California Marine Food and Game Fishes.* University of California Press, Berkeley, Los Angeles, London.

Hinton, Sam. 1987. *Seashore Life of Southern California.* University of California Press, Berkeley, Los Angeles, London.

Jameson, E. W. Jr., and Hans J. Peeters. 1988. *California Mammals.* University of California Press, Berkeley, Los Angeles, London.

Lincoln, Patricia G. 1985. "Pollinator Effectiveness and Ecology of Seed Set in *Cordylanthus maritimus* subsp. *maritimus* at Point Mugu, California." U.S. Fish and Wildlife Service, Endangered Species Office, Sacramento, CA.

Los Angeles Times, Metro Section. 7 June 1992.

Martin, Laura C. 1993. *The Folklore of Birds.* The Globe Pequot Press, Old Saybrook, CT.

McConnaughey, Bayard H., and Evelyn McConnaughey. 1985. *Pacific Coast.* Alfred A Knopf, New York.

National Park Service. 1982. "Draft Natural Resource Management Plan Environmental Assessment." Santa Monica Mountains National Recreation Area.

Onuf, Christopher P. 1987. *The Ecology of Mugu Lagoon, California: An Estuarine Profile.* U.S. Fish Wildlife Service. Biological Report 85(7.15).

Powell, Jerry A., and Charles L. Hogue. 1979. *California Insects.* Natural History Guides 44. University of California Press, Berkeley, Los Angeles, Oxford.

Ricketts, Edward F., Jack Calvin, and Joel W. Hedgpeth. 1985. *Between Pacific Tides.* Stanford University Press, Stanford.

San Francisco Bay National Wildlife Refuge. 1992. *Salt Marsh Manual.*

Scott, Shirley L., ed. 1987. *Field Guide to the Birds of North America.* National Geographic Society, Washington, D.C.

Sprunt, Alexander Jr. 1954. *Florida Bird Life.* Coward-McCann, Inc., New York.

Terres, John K. 1980. *The Audubon Society Encyclopedia of North American Birds.* Alfred A. Knopf, New York.

Zedler, Joy B. 1982. *The Ecology of Southern California Coastal Salt Marshes: A Community Profile.* U.S. Fish Wildlife Service. FWS/OBS-81.54.

Chapter 8

Applegate, Richard. 1975. The Datura Cult among the Chumash. *Journal of California Anthropology* 2(1):7-17.

Bean, Lowell John, and Charles R. Smith. 1978. Gabrielino. In Robert F. Heizer, ed. *Handbook of North American Indians,* vol. 8, *California,* pp. 538-549. Smithsonian Institution, Washington.

Blackburn, Thomas C. 1975. *December's Child. A Book of Chumash Oral Narratives.* University of California Press, Berkeley, Los Angeles, London.

Blackburn, Thomas C., and Kat Anderson. 1993. *Before the Wilderness.* Ballena Press, Menlo Park.

Chartkoff, Joseph L., and Kerry Kona Chartkoff. 1984. *The Archaeology of California.* Stanford University Press, Stanford, CA.

Erlandson, Jon M., and Roger H. Colten. 1991. *Hunter-Gatherers of Early Holocene Coastal California.* Institute of Archaeology, University of California, Los Angeles.

Gibson, Robert O. 1991. *The Chumash.* Chelsea House Publishers, New York, Philadelphia.

Gosline, William A., and Vernon E. Brock. 1971. *Handbook of Hawaiian Fishes.* University of Hawaii Press, Honolulu.

Heizer, R. F., and M. A. Whipple. 1971. *The California Indians.* University of California Press, Berkeley, Los Angeles, London.

Hudson, Travis, and Thomas Blackburn. 1982-1987. *The Material Culture of the Chumash Interaction Sphere.* 5 vols. Ballena Press, Menlo Park.

Johnston, Bernice Eastman. 1962. *California's Gabrieliño Indians.* Southwest Museum, Los Angeles.

King, Chester. 18 July 1994. *Prehistoric Native American Cultural Sites in the Santa Monica Mountains.* Topanga Anthropological Consultants, P.O. Box 826, Topanga, CA 90290.

McCall, Lynne, and Rosalind Perry, project coordinators. 1988. *California's Chumash Indians*. EZ Nature Books, San Luis Obispo, CA.

McCawley, William. 1996. *The First Angelinos: The Gabrielino Indians of Los Angeles*. Malki Museum Press/Ballena Press, Banning/Menlo Park.

Miller, Bruce W. 1988. *Chumash. A Picture of their World*. Sand River Press, 1319 14th Street, Los Osos, CA 93402.

Miller, Bruce W. 1991. *The Gabrielino*. Sand River Press, 1319 14th Street, Los Osos, CA 93402.

Chapter 9

Balls, Edward K. 1962. *Early Uses of California Plants*. University of California Press, Berkeley, Los Angeles, London.

Bowman, J. N. June 1957. Prominent Women of Provincial California. *The Historical Society of Southern California Quarterly* 39(2):149-166.

Clarke, Charlotte Bringle. 1977. *Edible and Useful Plants of California*. University of California Press, Berkeley, Los Angeles, London.

D'Andrea, Jeanne. 1982. *Ancient Herbs in the J. Paul Getty Museum Gardens*. The J. Paul Getty Museum, Malibu, CA.

Doyle, Thomas W., et al. 1985. *The Malibu Story*. Malibu Lagoon Museum, Malibu, CA.

Dudley, Leavitt. 1965. *Map of the Ranchos*. Title Insurance & Trust Co.

Jameson, E. W. Jr., and Hans J. Peeters. 1988. *California Mammals*. University of California Press, Berkeley, Los Angeles, London.

Neville, Sylvia Rindge Adamson. 1995. Interviews. Mrs. Neville is the daughter of Rhoda and Merritt Adamson.

Rogers, Betty. 1941. *Will Rogers*. University of Oklahoma Press, Norman, OK.

Sandmeier, Emil. 1995. Interviews. Sandmeier managed the Will Rogers ranch for many years.

Spengler, Walter. Undated. *Los Encinos. The Spring of Life*. Encino, CA.

Storer, Tracy I., and Lloyd P. Tevis Jr. 1955. *California Grizzly*. University of Nebraska Press, Lincoln, London.

Chapter 10

De Lisle, Harold, Gilbert Cantu, Jerrold Feldner, Paul O'Connor, Max Peterson, and Philip Brown. 1986. *The Distribution and Present Status of the Herpetofauna of the Santa Monica Mountains*. Southwestern Herpetologists Society.

Fuller, Thomas C., and Elizabeth McClintock.1986. *Poisonous Plants of California*. University of California Press, Berkeley, Los Angeles, London.

Hickman, James C., ed. 1993. *The Jepson Manual. Higher Plants of California*. University of California Press, London.

Hogue, Charles L. 1993. *Insects of the Los Angeles Basin*. Natural History Museum of Los Angeles County.

Jameson, E. W. Jr., and Hans J. Peeters. 1988. *California Mammals*. University of California Press, Berkeley, Los Angeles, London.

Los Angeles County Fire Department. October 1993. *Fire History*.

Los Angeles Times. Metro Section. 7 June 1992.

Martin, Laura C. 1993. *The Folklore of Birds*. The Globe Pequot Press, Old Saybrook, CT.

Stebbins, Robert C. 1985. *Western Reptiles and Amphibians*. Peterson Field Guide Series. Houghton Mifflin Company, Boston.

Stokes, Donald, and Lillian Stokes. 1979. *A Guide to Bird Behavior*. Little, Brown, Boston, Toronto, London.

Terres, John K. 1980. *The Audubon Society Encyclopedia of North American Birds*. Alfred A.

Knopf, New York.

Udvardy, Miklos D. F. 1977. *Field Guide to North American Birds, Western Region.* Alfred A. Knopf, New York.

Weathers, Wesley W. 1983. *Birds of Southern California's Deep Canyon.* University of California Press, Berkeley, Los Angeles, London.

Chapter 11

Bakker, Elna. 1984. *An Island Called California.* University of California Press, Berkeley, Los Angeles, London.

Barro, S. C., and S. G. Conard. 1991. Fire Effects on California Chaparral Systems: An Overview. *Environment International* 17:135-149.

Biswell, H. H., R. D. Taber, D. W. Hedrick, and A. M. Schultz. 1952. Management of Chamise Brushlands for Game in the North Coast Region of California. *California Fish and Game*, pp. 453-484.

Bullock, Stephen H. 1982. Life History and Seed Dispersal of *Dendromecon rigida*. In C. Eugene Conrad and Walter C. Oechel, tech. Coord. *Dynamics and Management of Mediterranean-Type Ecosystems*, p. 590. Pacific Southwest Forest and Range Experiment Station, General Technical Report PSW-58. Berkeley, CA.

Chew, Robert M., Bernard B. Butterworth, and Richard Grechman. 1959. The Effects of Fire on the Small Mammal Populations of Chaparral. *Journal of Mammalogy* 40:253.

Cook, Sherburne F. Jr. 1959. The Effects of Fire on a Population of Small Rodents. *Ecology* 40(1):102-108.

Dale, Nancy. 1986. *Flowering Plants of the Santa Monica Mountains, Coastal and Chaparral Regions of Southern California.* Capra Press, Santa Barbara, CA.

Davis, John. 1967. Some Effects of Deer Browsing on Chamise Sprouts after Fire. *The American Midland Naturalist* 77(1):234-238.

Evans, Arthur. 1993. Interviews. Curator of the Insect Zoo at the Natural History Museum of Los Angeles County.

Evans, William G. May/June, 1973. Fire Beetles and Forest Fires. *Insect World Digest*, pp. 14-18.

Franklin, Don, Los Angeles County Fire Department (retired). 1993-4. Interviews. Mr. Franklin fought the Kanan Fire.

Franklin, Scott E. April 1994. Chaparral Management Techniques: An Environmental Perspective. *Fire. Fremontia*, pp. 23-26. Reprints.

Garrett, Kimball, and Jon Dunn. 1981. *Birds of Southern California. Status and Distribution.* Los Angeles Audubon Society, Los Angeles, CA.

Jameson, E. W. Jr., and Hans J. Peeters. 1988. *California Mammals.* University of California Press, Berkeley, Los Angeles, London.

Kahn, Walter C. 1960. Observations on the Effect of a Burn on a Population of *Sceloporus occidentalis*. *Ecology* (April):358-359.

Keeley, Jon E. 1991. Seed Germination and Life History Syndromes in the California Chaparral. *The Botanical Review* (Apr-Jun):81-116. The New York Botanical Garden.

Keeley, Jon E., and Sterling C. Keeley. 1987. Chaparral. In Michael G. Barbour and William Dwight Billings, eds., *North American Terrestrial Vegetation*, pp. 165-207. Cambridge University Press, Cambridge, New York, New Rochelle, Melbourne, Sydney.

Lawrence, George E. 1966. Ecology of Vertebrate Animals in Relation to Chaparral Fire in theSierra Nevada Foothills. *Ecology* 47(2):278-291.

Los Angeles County Fire Department, Battalion 5. 1993. Brush Clearance in Coastal Malibu. Memo.

Los Angeles Times. 17 November, 1993. P.E2, Col. 6.

Los Angeles Times. 24-26 October 1978. Reports on Kanan Fire, bylined Ellen Hume, Bruce Keppel, Robert Kistler, Penelope McMillan, Bella Stumbo, Ted Thackrey Jr., and Dorothy Townsend.

Mills, James M. 1986. Herbivores and Early Postfire Succession in Southern California Chaparral. *Ecology* 67(6):1637-1649.

Moldenke, Andrew R. 1977. Insect-Plant Relations. In Norman J. W. Thrower and David E. Bradbury, eds. *Chile-California Mediterranean Scrub Atlas*, pp. 199-217. Dowden, Hutchinson and Ross, Inc., Stroudsburg, PA.

Newton, Jim, and Shawn Hubler. November 6, 1993. 19 Southland Fires Called Suspicious. *Los Angeles Times.*

O'Leary, John F. 1988. Habitat Differentiation among Herbs in Postburn Californian Chaparral and Coastal Sage Scrub. *American Midland Naturalist* 120(1):41-49.

Pierpont, Captain Don. 1993. Interview. Vegetation Management Officer of the Los Angeles County Fire Department.

Quinn, Ronald D. 1990. *Habitat Preferences and Distribution of Mammals in California Chaparral.* Research Paper PSW-202. Pacific Southwest Research Station, Berkeley, CA.

Quinn, Ronald D. 1979. Effects of Fire on Small Mammals in the Chaparral. In D. L. Koch, ed. *Proceedings, California-Nevada Wildlife Transactions,* pp. 125-133.

Radtke, Klaus W.-H., Arthur M. Arndt, and Ronald H. Wakimoto. 1982. Fire History of the Santa Monica Mountains. In *Dynamics and Management of Mediterranean-Type Ecosystems*, Gen. Tech. Rep. PSW-58, pp. 438-443. Pacific Southwest Forest and Range Experiment Station, Berkeley, CA.

Radtke, Klaus. Dr. Radtke supplied the map of the Kanan fire.

Rogers, Michael J. 1982. Fire Management in Southern California. In *Dynamics and Management of Mediterranean-Type Ecosystems*, Gen. Tech. Rep. PSW-58, pp. 496-501. Pacific Southwest Forest and Range Experiment Station, Berkeley, CA.

Stassforth, Margaret. 1993-4. Interviews. Stassforth is studying effects of chaparral management techniques.

Stebbins, Robert C. 1985. *Western Reptiles and Amphibians.* Peterson Field Guide Series. Houghton Mifflin Company, Boston.

Terres, John K. 1980. *The Audubon Society Encyclopedia of North American Birds.* Alfred A. Knopf, New York.

Whitney, Stephen. 1979. *The Sierra Nevada.* Sierra Club Books, San Francisco.

Wirtz, William O. II. 1977. Vertebrate Post-fire Succession. In *Environmental Consequences of Fire and Fuel Management in Mediterranean Ecosystems*, pp. 46-57. USDA Forest Service, General Technical Report WO-3.

Chapter 12

Department of Regional Planning. 29 December 1981. *The Malibu/Santa Monica Mountains Interim Area Plan.* County of Los Angeles.

Edelman, Paul. December 1990. *Critical Wildlife Corridor/Habitat Linkage Areas between the Santa Susana Mountains, the Simi Hills and the Santa Monica Mountains.* The Santa Monica Mountains Conservancy, 3700 Solstice Canyon Road, Malibu, CA 90265.

Lieberstein, Terry Ann. May 1989. *Reserve Design in the Santa Monica Mountains.* Master's thesis. California State University, Northridge.

Santa Monica Mountains Conservancy. April 1990. *Preserving the Critical Link: A Discussion of the Wildlife Corridor from the Santa Susana Mountains*

to the Santa Monica Mountains via the Simi Hills.
State of California.

Santa Monica Mountains National Recreation Area.
10 April 1995. "Memorandum of Understanding
between National Park Service and California
Department of Parks and Recreation and Santa
Monica Mountains Conservancy for the
Cooperative Management of the Santa Monica
Mountains National Recreation Area."

Santa Monica Mountains National Recreation Area.
July 1993. *Zuma-Trancas Canyons Development
Concept Plan.* National Park Service.

Santa Monica Mountains National Recreation Area.
January 1987. *Addendum to the Land Protection
Plan.* National Park Service.

Santa Monica Mountains National Recreation Area.
1980. *Historical Overview of the Santa Monica
Mountains.* National Park Service.

Santa Monica Mountains National Recreation Area.
Undated. *Statement of National Significance.*
National Park Service.

UCLA Extension. March 1994. *The 101 Corridor:
Land-Use Planning and Intergovernmental
Relations.* UCLA.

Wayne, Robert K., Todd K. Fuller, et al. November
1995. " The Distribution and Status of Large
Carnivores in the Santa Monica Mountains
National Recreation Area. Cooperative Research
Proposal to the National Park Service." UCLA.

Index

A

Adamson family 137-139
Adamson House 133, 138
Adamson, Merritt 138
Adamson, Rhoda 139
Adenostema fasciculatum, chamise 6, 49, 50, 156
Adenostema sparsifolium, red shank 53, 54
Adiantum capillus-veneris, venus maidenhair fern 98, 99
Allen, Larry 108, 109
Amaranthus sp., pigweed 61
Ammonite 30
Ant, California harvester *(Pogonomyrex californicus)* 67-68, 69, 169
Anthidium edwardsii, resin bee 117
Anthocharis sara, sara orange-tip butterfly 62, 65
Anthophora urbana, digger bee 63, 65
Aphelocoma coerulescens, scrub jay 44, 79, 80
Aphid 65
Aphonopelmus eutylenum, tarantula 72, 73
Apis mellifera, European honeybee 45, 65

Aplysia californica, brown sea-hare 117
Archilestes californica, California archilestes damselfly 98, 103
Archytas apicifer, tachinid fly 144, 149
Arctostaphylos eastwoodii, Eastwood manzanita 168-169
Athene cunicularia, burrowing owl 90
Atlides halesus, great purple hairstreak butterfly 83, 84
Atriplex sp., saltbush 61

B

Barkley, Dr. Linda 55
Bassariscus astutus, ringtail 103, 105
Bat, canyon *(Pipistrellus hesperus)* 55, 69
Bat, long-eared *(Myotis evotis)* 9
Bear, grizzly *(Ursus arctos)* 130
Bee, digger *(Anthophora urbana)* 63, 65
Bee, resin *(Anthidium edwardsii)* 117
Beefly, greater *(Bombylius major)*, 61, 63, 65
Bees, native 45, 63, 65, 117
Beetle, brown rain *(Pleocoma badia)* 41
Beetle, western fire *(Melanophila occi-*

dentalis) 161
Bellamy, Chuck 161
Bird's beak, salt marsh *(Cordylanthus maritimus)* 117
Bobcat *(Lynx rufus)* 95, 98, 105
Boletus dryophilus, red-capped bolete mushroom 82, 84
Bombus vosnesenskii, yellow-faced bumblebee 5, 45, 46
Bombycilla cedrorum, cedar waxwing 43, 44, 91
Bombylius major, greater beefly 61, 63, 65
Bonito (Skipjack) *(Katsuwonus pelamis)* 124
Bothriocyrtum californicum, trapdoor spider 80
Brephidium exile, pygmy blue butterfly 58, 61
Broom, scale *(Lepidospartum squamatum)* 70, 73
Buckwheat, California *(Eriogonum fasciculatum)* 46, 64, 65, 72
Bueller, Mark 36, 80
Bumblebee, yellow-faced *(Bombus vosne-*

senskii) 5, 45, 46

Bushtit *(Psaltriparus minimus)* 152-153

Buteo jamaicensis, red-tailed hawk 125, 161, 168, 171

Butorides striatus, green-backed heron

Butterfly, buckeye *(Junonia coenia)* 86-87, 89

Butterfly, Comstock's fritillary *(Speyeria callippe comstocki)* 85, 88

Butterfly, great purple hairstreak *(Atlides halesus)* 83, 84

Butterfly, pygmy blue *(Brephidium exile)* 58, 61

Butterfly, sara orange-tip *(Anthocharis sara)* 62, 65

Butterfly, variable checkerspot *(Euphydryas chalcedona)* 4, 6

C

Callianassa californiensis, ghost shrimp 114, 115

Callipepla californica, California quail 52, 53, 80, 166

Callirhytis quercuspomiformis, oak gall wasp 85

Calypte anna, Anna's hummingbird 42, 44, 49

Calypte costae, Costa's hummingbird 61

Camissonia cheiranthifolia, beach primrose 115, 116

Camouflage 7, 8, 54, 68, 95, 104, 127

Canis familiaris, domestic dog 141, 145, 148, 173, 174

Canis latrans, coyote 41, 44, 48, 81, 141-142, 148, 160-161

Castilleja affinis, indian paintbrush 49, 51

Cat, domestic *(Felis cattus)* 141-142, 149, 152

Catocala piatrix, walnut underwing moth 7, 8

Ceanothus sp. 39, 41

Ceanothus, big pod *(Ceanothus megacarpus)*
27, 44, 45

Ceanothus, greenbark *(Ceanothus spinosus)* 45

Ceanothus megacarpus, big-pod ceanothus 27, 44, 45

Ceanothus spinosus, greenbark ceanothus 45

Cerithidea californica, California hornsnail 113

Chamaea fasciata, wrentit 49, 52, 156

Chamise *(Adenostema fasciculatum)* 6, 49, 50, 156

Chaparral ecosystems 38-55

Charadrius alexandrinus, snowy plover 115-116

Cherry, holly-leaf *(Prunus ilicifolia)* 125

Chia *(Salvia columbaria)* 70, 72, 123

Chingüchngech, Gabrielino and Fernandeño god 123, 126

Chumash 15, 119-120, 122-123, 124-125

Clam, California glass mya *(Cryptomya californica)* 114-115

Climate 30-36

Cnemidophorus tigris, whiptail lizard 67

Cockroach, American *(Periplaneta americana)* 144, 149

Colaptes auratus cafer, northern flicker 143-145, 146

Cold Creek 99

Commensalism 6, 53, 114-115, 149, 153

Cordylanthus maritimus, salt marsh bird's beak 117

Coreopsis gigantaea, giant coreopsis 21, 59, 61, 68

Coreopsis, giant *(Coreopsis gigantaea)* 21, 59, 61, 68

Cortaderia selloana, pampas grass 7, 9

Corvus corax, common raven 161, 168

Coyote *(Canis latrans)* 41, 44, 48, 81, 141-142, 148, 160-161

Crespi, Padre Juan 9-10, 15, 36

Crotalus viridis, Pacific rattlesnake 48, 49

Cryptomya californica, California glass
mya clam 114-115

Ctenucha brunnea, ctenucha moth 71, 73

D

Damselfly, California archilestes *(Archilestes californica)* 98, 103

Datura meteloides, Momoy or Jimson Weed 125

Deer, mule *(Odocoileus hemionus)* 77, 80, 87, 90, 161, 164

Deer weed *(Lotus scoparius)* 63, 65

Delphinium cardinale, scarlet larkspur 169, 171

Dendromecon rigida, bush poppy 169

Dicentra ochroleuca, fireheart 169

Dipodomys agilis, Pacific kangaroo rat 69, 72, 73, 160, 166, 168

Dispersal 6-7, 44, 49, 67, 80, 84, 91, 102

Dog, domestic *(Canis familiaris)* 141, 145, 148, 173, 174

Dowitcher, long-billed *(Limnodromus scolopaceus)* 113

E

Earthquake 25

Eck, Arthur 176

Ecosystem 3-23, 26, 28, 30, 31, 33, 34-35

Edelman, Paul 174

Edmiston, Joe 174, 177

Encelia californica, bush sunflower 66, 67, 68

Encino, city of 17, 125, 130

Encino, Spanish name for coast live oak 17

Enkema, Pat 112-113, 116-117

Eriogonum fasciculatum, California buckwheat 46, 64, 65, 72

Eschscholzia californica, California poppy 167, 168

Euphydryas chalcedona, variable checkerspot butterfly 4, 6

Evans, Dr. Arthur 41, 73, 162

F

Falco peregrinus, peregrine falcon 109, 112
Falcon, peregrine *(Falco peregrinus)* 109, 112
Felis cattus, domestic cat 141-142, 149, 152
Felis concolor, mountain lion 6, 7, 87, 90, 173, 174
Fern, venus maidenhair *(Adiantum capillus-veneris)* 98, 99
Fernandeño 15, 119, 122, 123-124, 125-127
Fire 15, 34-35, 76, 81, 124, 125, 154-171
Fire, Kanan 154-171
Fireheart, *Dicentra ochroleuca,* 169
Flicker, northern *(Colaptes auratus cafer)* 143-145, 146
Flood 31-32, 98, 165
Flower color and pollinators 49, 65
Fly, tachinid *(Archytas apicifer)* 144, 149
Fog 35-36, 135, 137
Fossils 19, 29, 30
Fox, gray *(Urocyon cinereoargentus)* 55, 155, 157
Fox, red *(Vulpes vulpes)* 148, 150
Franklin, Don 155, 156, 169
Fresh water ecosystems 92-105

G

Gabrielino 15, 119, 120, 122
Garnier (building) 130, 131
Garnier, Eugene 130-131, 134-135
Geococcyx californianus, roadrunner 69
Geology 24-26, 28-30
Gerris remigis, water strider 104, 105
Godwit, marbled *(Limosa fedoa)* 113-114
Gopher, pocket *(Thomomys bottae)* 168
Grass, native 81, 87
Grass, pampas (& jubata grass) *(Cortaderia selloana)* 7, 9
Grassland 81, 85-87, 91
Griffith Park 11, 22
Grosbeak, black-headed *(Pheucticus melanocephalus)* 169, 171
Ground squirrel, California *(Spermophilus beecheyi)* 81, 85-86, 90
Gull, California *(Larus californicus)* 107
Gull, ring-billed *(Larus delawarensis)* 107
Gull, western *(Larus occidentalis)* 107

H

Haliotis rufescens, abalone shell 121, 122
Hawk, red-tailed *(Buteo jamaicensis)* 125, 161, 168, 171
Heron, green-backed *(Butorides striatus)* 101, 105
Heteromeles arbutifolia, Toyon 14, 15, 43, 44
Hippodamia convergens, convergent lady-bug 65, 161
Holly, California (see Toyon)
Honeybee, European *(Apis mellifera)* 45, 65
Hornsnail, California *(Cerithidea californica)* 113
Humaliwo 15, 118, 122
Hummingbird, Anna's *(Calypte anna)* 42, 44, 49
Hummingbird, Costa's *(Calypte costae)* 61
Hyalophora euryalus, ceanothus silk moth 47, 49
Hyla (see *Pseudacris)*

I

Icterus cuculatus, hooded oriole 147, 148
Inbreeding 7, 173-174
Interaction 3-9
Introduced species 9, 141-142, 144-145, 147, 148-149, 150, 151, 152, 153
Ivy, German *(Senecio mikanioides)* 151, 153
Ixodes pacificus, deer tick 44

J

Jay, scrub *(Aphelocoma coerulescens)* 44, 79, 80
Jimson weed or Momoy *(Datura meteloides)* 125
Johnny jump-up *(Viola pedunculata)* 83, 85
Junonia coenia, buckeye butterfly 86-87, 89

K

Kangaroo rat, Pacific *(Dipodomys agilis)* 69, 72, 73, 160, 166, 168
Kats, Dr. Lee 67, 93, 103, 104
Katsuwonus pelamis, bonito or skipjack 124
Keeney, Tom 112, 115
Kelp, giant perennial *(Macrocystis* sp.) 116
Kingsnake, mountain *(Lampropeltis zonata pulchra)* 100, 103

L

Lactation 53
Ladybug, convergent *(Hippodamia convergens)* 65, 161
Lampropeltis zonata pulchra, mountain kingsnake 100, 103
Landslide 19, 21, 30, 31-32, 139
Larkspur, scarlet *(Delphinium cardinale)* 169, 171
Larus californicus, California gull 107
Larus delawarensis, ring-billed gull 107
Larus occidentalis, western gull 107
Las Virgines, origin of name 22
Lepidospartum squamatum, scale broom 70, 73
Lieberstein, Terry Ann 174
Lilac, wild (see *Ceanothus)*
Lilium humboldti, Humboldt lily 97, 102
Lily, Humboldt *(Lilium humboldti)* 97, 102
Limnodromus scolopaceus, long-billed dowitcher 113
Limosa fedoa, marbled godwit 113-114

Lion, mountain *(Felis concolor)* 6, 7, 87, 90, 173, 174

Lizard, side-blotched *(Uta stansburiana)* 41, 44, 160

Lizard, western fence *(Sceloporus occidentalis)* 35

Lizard, horned *(Phrynosoma coronatum)* 68, 149, 152

Lizard, whiptail *(Cnemidophorus tigris)* 67

Los Angeles Basin 11, 14, 15

Lotus scoparius, deer weed 63, 65

Lynx rufus, bobcat 95, 98, 105

M

Macrocystis sp., giant perennial kelp 116

Malibu, origin of name 15

Malibu Canyon Boulevard 21-22

Malibu Creek 36-37

Malibu Creek State Park 18, 19, 22, 175

Malibu Lagoon 11, 107, 108-109, 110, 111, 112-113, 116-117

Manzanita, Eastwood *(Arctostaphylos eastwoodii)* 168-169

Marine ecosystems 106-117

Masticophis lateralis, California striped racer snake 54

Meadowlark, western *(Sturnella neglecta)* 86, 91

Melanerpes formicivorus, acorn woodpecker 77, 79,-80, 84-85

Melanophilia occidentalis, western fire beetle 161

Mimicry 6, 8, 127

Mistletoe *(Phoradendron sp.)* 80, 91

Mite, water (Hydrachnellae family) 102

Momoy or Jimson weed *(Datura meteloides)* 125

Moth, ceanothus silk *(Hyalophora euryalus)* 47, 49

Moth, ctenucha *(Ctenucha brunnea)* 71, 73

Moth, hornet *(Synanthodon robiniae)* 6, 8

Moth, MacDunnough's leafwing *(Pero macdunnoughi)* 54

Moth, walnut underwing *(Catocala piatrix)* 7, 8

Moth, yucca *(Tegeticula maculata)* 61

Mouse, brush *(Peromyscus boylii)* 166

Mouse, California *(Peromyscus californicus)* 6, 53-54

Mugu, origin of name 15

Mugu Lagoon 11, 15, 106, 109, 112, 113-116, 117

Mulholland Drive and Highway 17-18

Mulholland, William 17

Mushroom, red-capped bolete *(Boletus dryophilus)* 82, 84

Mutualism 6, 61, 84

Muwu 15, 124-125

Mycorrhiza 84

Myotis evotis, long-eared bat 9

N

National Recreation Area (Santa Monica Mountains) 23, 175, 176

Neotoma fuscipes, dusky-footed woodrat 6, 53-54, 55, 84, 160, 164

Newt, California *(Taricha torosa)* 93, 98-99, 104-105

O

Oak, coast live *(Quercus agrifolia)* 17, 19, 76, 80, 81, 84, 85, 163, 165

Oak, coastal scrub *(Quercus dumosa)* 60

Oak, valley *(Quercus lobata)* 17, 18, 90, 91, 143

Oak woodland ecosystems 74-80, 81-85

Odocoileus hemionus, mule deer 77, 80, 87, 90, 161, 164

Olivella biplicata, purple olive snail 114, 116

Oriole, hooded *(Icterus cuculatus)* 147, 148

Owl, burrowing *(Athene cunicularia)* 90

P

Pacific Coast Highway (PCH) 19-20, 21

Pacific High 30, 31

Paintbrush, indian *(Castilleja affinis)* 49, 51

Palm, California fan *(Washingtonia filifera)* 147, 148

Parasite 4, 6, 63-65, 84, 85, 102, 113

Parasitoid 6, 63, 65

PCH (see Pacific Coast Highway)

Pepsis sp., tarantula hawk wasp

Periplaneta americana, American cockroach 144, 149

Pero macdunnoughi, MacDunnough's leafwing moth 54

Peromyscus boylii, brush mouse 166

Peromyscus californicus, California mouse 6, 53-54

Petaloconchus montereyensi, little fixed snail 112-113

Phacelia, Parry's *(Phacelia parryi)* 167, 168

Phacelia parryi, Parry's phacelia 167, 168

Phalaenoptilus nuttalli, common poorwill *141*

Pheucticus melanocephalus, black-headed grosbeak 169, 171

Phoca vitulina, harbor seal 108, 109

Phoradendron sp., mistletoe 80, 91

Phrynosoma coronatum, horned lizard 68, 149, 152

Pickleweed *(Salicornia virginiana)* 115, 117

Pigweed *(Amaranthus sp.)* 61

Pipistrellus hesperus, canyon bat 55, 69

Pituophis melanoleucus, gopher snake 84, 86

Pleocoma badia, brown rain beetle 41

Plover, snowy *(Charadrius alexandrinus)* 115-116

Pogonomyrex californicus, California harvester ant 67-68, 69, 169

Point Mugu State Park 20

Poison oak *(Toxicodendron diver-*

silobum) 94

Pollution 37, 175

Poorwill, common *(Phalaenoptilus nuttalli)* 141

Poppy, California *(Eschscholzia californica)* 167. 168

Poppy, bush *(Dendromecon rigida)* 169

Predation 6, 9, 41, 44, 54, 55, 80, 81, 86, 87, 90, 94, 95, 103, 104-105, 109, 112, 113-114, 117, 124, 125-127, 141, 148, 149, 152, 166, 168

Preece, Dan 173

Primrose, beach *(Camissonia cheiranthifolia)* 115, 116

Prunus ilicifolia, holly-leaf cherry 125

Psaltriparus minimus, bushtit 152-153

Pseudacris cadaverina, California treefrog 102, 104

Pseudacris regilla, Pacific treefrog 94, 95

Q

Quail, California *(Callipepla californica)* 52-53, 80, 166

Quercus agrifolia, coast live oak 17, 19, 76, 80, 81, 84, 85, 163, 165

Quercus dumosa, coastal scrub oak 60

Quercus lobata, valley oak 17, 18, 90, 91, 143

R

Rabbit, Audubon's cottontail *(Sylvilagus auduboni)* 81

Rabbit, brush *(Sylvilagus bachmani)* 87, 90, 160

Rail, light-footed clapper *(Rallus longirostris levipes)* 148

Rainfall 31-33

Rallus longirostris levipes, light-footed clapper rail 148

Ranch, (Will Rogers') Santa Monica 132, 134, 135, 137

Rancho Guadalasca 129-130

Rancho los Encinos 130-131

Rancho Topanga-Malibu-Sequit 2, 9

Rattlesnake, Pacific *(Crotalus viridis)* 48, 49

Raven, common *(Corvus corax)* 161, 168

Red shank *(Adenostema sparsifolium)* 53, 54

Reproduction 41, 53, 61, 63, 69, 84, 95, 98, 102, 103, 109, 115, 117, 169, 173-174

Rindge, Frederick 9, 19, 137

Ringtail *(Bassariscus astutus)* 103, 105

Roadrunner *(Geococcyx californianus)* 69

Robin, American *(Turdus migratorius)* 6, 44, 169

Rogers, Betty 135-137

Rogers, Will 135-137

S

Sage, black *(Salvia mellifera)* 65

Sage, Cleveland *(Salvia clevelandii)* 5

Sage scrub ecosystems 56-73

Sakamoto, Louise 48, 85

Salicornia virginiana, pickleweed 115, 117

Saltbush *(Atriplex* sp.) 61

Salvia clevelandii, Cleveland sage 5

Saliva columbaria, chia 70,72, 123

Salvia mellifera, black sage 65

San Andreas Fault 24, 25-26

San Fernando Valley 15-17

Santa Ana wind 33-35, 117, 155

Santa Monica, origin of name 9-10

Santa Monica Mountains Conservancy 174-175, 176

Sauvajot, Ray 81

Sceloporus occidentalis, western fence lizard 35

Schwartz, Steve 175

Sciurus griseus, gray squirrel 77, 78, 80

Sciurus niger, fox squirrel 152, 153

Sea lettuce *(Ulva lactuca)* 111, 112

Sea-hare, brown *(Aplysia californica)* 117

Seal, harbor *(Phoca vitulina)* 108, 109

Senecio mikanioides, German ivy 151, 153

Sepulveda Canyon 28

Sepulveda pass 28, 36

Sexual interaction 7, 41, 48, 49, 65, 67, 95, 98-99, 102, 103, 105, 117, 125

Shell, abalone *(Haliotis rufescens)* 122

Shell, olivella 114, 116, 119-120

Shrimp, ghost *(Callianassa californiensis)* 114, 115

Siutcanga 125-127

Sky Coyote (Chumash god) 123

Snail, purple olive *(Olivella biplicata)* 114, 116

Snail, little fixed *(Petaloconchus montereyensis)* 112-113

Snake, California striped racer *(Masticophis lateralis)* 54

Snake, gopher *(Pituophis melanoleucus)* 84, 86

Snake, two-striped garter *(Thamnophis hammondi)* 143

Sparrow, white-crowned *(Zonotrichia leucophrys)* 87, 91

Spermophilus beecheyi, California ground squirrel 81, 85-86, 90

Speyeria callippe comstocki, Comstock's fritillary butterfly 85, 88

Spider, trapdoor *(Bothriocyrtum californicum)* 80

Squirrel, fox *(Sciurus niger)* 152, 153

Squirrel, gray *(Sciurus griseus)* 77, 78, 80

Starling, European *(Sturnus vulgaris)* 142, 144-145

Stassforth, Margaret 168

Streams 30-31, 36-37, 92

Sturnella neglecta, western meadowlark 86, 91

Sturnus vulgaris, European starling 142, 144-145

Sun (Chumash god) 31, 123

Sunflower, bush *(Encelia californica)* 66,

67, 68

Sylvilagus auduboni, Audubon's cotton-tail rabbit 81

Sylvilagus bachmani, brush rabbit 87, 90, 160

Synanthodon robiniae, hornet moth 6, 8

T

Tarantula *(Aphonopelmus eutylenum)* 72, 73

Taricha torosa, California newt 93, 98-99, 104-105

Tegeticula maculata, yucca moth 61

Temperature 33

Thamnophis hammondi, two-striped garter snake 143

Thomomys bottae, pocket gopher 168

Thomas, Tim 174

Tick, deer *(Ixodes pacificus)* 44

Tidepools 110, 112-113, 116-117

Tomol 124-125

Topanga State Park 20-21, 175

Topanga Canyon Boulevard 20, 21

Topanga, origin of name 15

Topography 10-11, 17-18

Toxicodendron diversilobum, poison oak 94

Toyon (Spanish name for California holly), *(Heteromeles arbutifolia)* 14, 15, 43, 44

Tree, California bay *(Umbellularia californica)* 94

Treefrog, California *(Pseudacris cadaverina)* 102, 104

Treefrog, Pacific *(Pseudacris regilla)* 94, 95

Turdus migratorius, American robin 6, 44, 169

U

Ulva lactuca, sea lettuce 111, 112

Umbellularia californica, California bay tree 94

Urocyon cinereoargentus, gray fox 55, 155, 157

Ursus arctos, grizzly bear 130

Uta stansburiana, side-blotched lizard 41, 44, 160

V

Valentine, Mary 54, 65, 73, 86, 99

Valley oak savannah ecosystems 74, 90-91

Viola pedunculata, Johnny jump-up 83, 85

Vulpes vulpes, red fox 148, 150

W

Washingtonia filifera, California fan palm 147, 148

Wasp, trantula hawk *(Pepsis* sp.) 70, 73

Wasp, oak gall *(Callirhytis quercuspomiformis)* 85

Water strider *(Gerris remigis)* 104, 105

Waxwing, cedar *(Bombycilla cedrorum)* 43, 44, 91

Wetlands 11, 106-117

Wildlife links 174-175, 176

Wilson, Jan 49, 52

Woodpecker, acorn *(Melanerpes formicivorus)* 77, 79-80, 84-85

Woodrat, dusky-footed *(Neotoma fuscipes)* 6, 53-54, 55, 84, 160, 164

Wrentit *(Chamaea fasciata)* 49, 52, 156

Y

Yucca whipplei, Whipple's yucca 61

Yucca, Whipple's *(Yucca whipplei)* 61

Z

Zonotrichia leucophrys, white-crowned sparrow 87, 91

Photography Credits

AR	Art Roach		RG	Rosser Garrison
BS	Brad Sillasen		RS	Ray Sauvajot
CH	C.L. Hogue		SBHS	Courtesy, Santa Barbara Historical Society (unknown photographer)
DF	Don Frack			
DS	Dennis Sheridan		SBMNH	Rick Terry, Courtesy, Santa Barbara Museum of Natural History
HC	Herbert Clarke			
HP	Courtesy, Hans Peeters			
JL	Jack Levy		SRAN	Courtesy, Sylvia Rindge Adamson Neville
JM	Jerry Meehan			
JVZM	Detail from a painting by Julie Van Zandt May in the Malibu Lagoon Museum		SU	Sandra Uchitel
			SWHS	Courtesy, Southwestern Herpetologists Society
KR	Based on a map by Klaus Radtke		SWM	Courtesy, Southwest Museum (unknown photographer)
LS	Larry Sansone			
MP	Moose Peterson, Wildlife Research Photography		WDS	Courtesy, Weather Data Systems
			WRM	Courtesy, Will Rogers Memorial
NPS	Courtesy, National Park Service		WS	Walter Spengler
PM	Paul Morse, Los Angeles Times Syndicate			

All other photography by Margaret Huffman